eating the greek way

more than 100 fresh and delicious recipes
from some of the healthiest people in the world

fedon alexander lindberg, m.d.

Clarkson Potter/Publishers
New York

This book contains general information about the author's dietary approach, based on a traditional Greek diet, and includes more than a hundred Mediterranean-inspired recipes. It is not intended as a substitute for the advice and care of your physician, and as with any other diet or nutrition plan, you should use proper discretion, in consultation with your physician, in utilizing the information presented. The author and the publisher expressly disclaim responsibility for any adverse effects that may result from the use or application of the information contained in this book.

With special thanks to Per Lauritz Lien, our wonderful and creative chef at the clinic in Oslo, who helped me create and test many of the recipes, to the delight of our "test panel." I would also like to thank my "Norwegian mom" Wera, for her unbeatable chocolate cake recipe; Mats Widén for his beautiful photography and wonderful memories of our trip to Greece; my superb editor Maggie Ramsay, and all those who have contributed to this book. It has been a pleasure.

Contents

Introduction

It is dark outside; only the stars give out a gentle light this moonless summer night. The air is warm and dry, and the whole family—parents, grandparents, and siblings—is sitting outside, around the large dinner table on the veranda of our summer home. The enticing smell of sea bream and octopus cooking on the grill competes with the delicate scent of gardenia and jasmine from the garden. The table is covered with countless little dishes of meze: Greek salad with feta cheese and oregano, lima beans in tomato sauce, calamari, prawns, lamb meatballs with mint and anise, the obligatory tzatziki, stuffed grape leaves, chickpea croquettes…

This idyllic evening reminds me of when I was growing up in Greece in the late sixties and early seventies. Life was definitely much simpler then. There were no mobile phones, no internet; there may have been fewer choices but there was also less pressure and more time to spend with family and friends. Nowadays we have more material goods than ever, but few of us are content. We may live longer, but that is mostly thanks to expensive medicines and advanced medical technology, not because of a better lifestyle. We live stressful lives struggling to meet all our commitments, we undertake little or no physical activity and much of the food we eat is denatured and highly processed. We manage, nonetheless, to achieve and experience more than previous generations could have imagined. But are we happier or healthier?

Greeks, like many other Mediterranean people, have always been very fond of good food and recognized how important it is as part of a happy, healthy life. As far back as the 4th century BC, some

2,500 years ago, Archestratos, from the Greek colony of Syracuse, was busy writing the world's first cookbook, *Gastronomia*. In it, he described in detail not only a great number of recipes, but also ingredients and where they could be bought. He knew which fish could be found in the markets of Carthago or Pella and where to find the best bakers in Athens. He thought highly of eel from the Kopais lake near Athens (now dried up), wine from the islands of Thassos and Lesbos, and fried sardines from Faliron on the coast of Athens. It is fascinating to read about these ancient food markets and it is clear that there was an abundant and varied supply of foods from the Mediterranean and Black Sea. However, what is just as interesting is that the social aspect of eating and drinking with family and friends was at least as important as the food itself.

It seems the ancient Greeks had a clear understanding of the real meaning of the "good life," though perhaps this is hardly surprising given that Greece produced Dionysus, the god of wine and feasting, and Hippocrates, the Father of Medicine (and the man who coined the expression "Let food be thy medicine"). Hippocrates realized that all disease has a physiological and rational explanation and, contrary to what was once believed, was not the work of the gods! This meant that man had a hand in his own destiny—adequate rest, eating healthily, fresh air, and cleanliness would help prevent and cure disease. What these two contrasting "personalities" represent, I believe, offers us an example of the balance that is needed in order to maintain physical and mental health and well-being. The ancient Greek tradition of celebrating Dionysus was an expression of their love for life and the joy of good food and drink enjoyed with good company. The Hippocratic understanding of how food can prevent and cure disease illustrated their appreciation of wellness and a healthy life. If you add to that equation the ancient Greeks' belief in "everything in moderation" and "a sound mind in a sound body" you have a well balanced and simple philosophy of life; one that is just as applicable today as it was in ancient times.

Which foods are most beneficial to our health? There's no simple answer to that, but the Mediterranean diet has long been acclaimed as one of the healthiest in the world. Olive oil, garlic, wine, fish, yogurt, cheese, nuts, legumes, whole grains, fruits, and lots of vegetables are the key ingredients. There is of course no single "Mediterranean diet;" it varies from region to region. The traditional diet of the Greek island of Crete has been specifically recognized for its health benefits, explaining the long life expectancy and low risk of heart disease and cancer among the island's population. The best scientific evidence for these health benefits was presented at a large international conference back in 1993, sponsored in part by Harvard University. The traditional Cretan diet is relatively high in fat, accounting for around 40 percent of total energy, unlike the diets of many Western countries that succumbed to the low-fat craze of recent decades. However, most of the fat in the Cretan diet comes from natural, minimally processed sources like olive oil and nuts, and is mainly monounsaturated fat. A substantial body of scientific evidence suggests that it would be wise to greatly reduce the amount of sugar and refined starchy foods—such as white

bread, pasta, rice, and potatoes—in the typical Western diet, and instead eat more healthy fat from plants and fish. Greek cuisine can be a great source of inspiration for moving in that direction. My dietary approach, described in detail in my first book, *The Greek Doctor's Diet*, is based on the traditional Cretan diet, but updated and revised to take account of the latest information on the Glycemic Index (GI) and Glycemic Load (GL). (The former is a method of ranking foods according to how quickly they raise the blood sugar, while the latter takes account of the effect of the amount of carbohydrates we actually eat.) The recipes in this book are based on that diet. They are not designed to be used as a means to short-term weight loss, but as part of a new and better way of eating for life.

Creating the book you hold in your hands has been a delightful project for me. Going back to my roots and traveling in Greece in May was, as always, a wonderful experience, and rather different from what the majority of tourists experience at the height of the season in mid summer. The temperature is just right, everything is green and in bloom and the incredible scent of flowers is everywhere; plus the locals are laid back and not yet tired of the hordes of tourists who "invade" their territory during the summer. Some unforgettable days and nights were spent working on this book in Athens, and on Santorini and Cephalonia, and if even just a little of the enjoyment and love of good food and good company that our team enjoyed comes across in these pages then you will begin to understand the simple pleasure I felt enjoying home-cooked food on that veranda under the stars.

Food, health, and weight

Eating the Greek Way is an easy-to-follow approach to cooking and eating that can significantly affect the way you feel—as well as the way you look. The tempting recipes in this book reinvigorate familiar ingredients—such as juicy ripe tomatoes, creamy feta cheese, aromatic olive oil, hearty chickpeas, and fresh fish—in irresistible yet simple recipes. The beauty of *Eating the Greek Way* is that every tantalizing meal in the pages that follow—from Grilled Chicken with Garlic and Almond Sauce to Cinnamon Parfaits with Marinated Berries—can help you lose weight and improve your health. The recipes are based on a nutritional concept that you can and should follow for the rest of your life. It does not rely on calorie counting or food restrictions, so you will probably not eat less, just differently from the way you are used to. This way of eating is based on great-tasting natural foods that will increase well-being and vitality.

The food you eat can contribute in a negative or positive way to your health and quality of life, so it is essential to make wise choices with regard to both the type and amount of the various foods you consume. And that is what this cookbook is all about—making delicious food choices in order to restore a more natural balance of the types of carbohydrates, proteins, and fats you eat and to meet the body's needs for important vitamins, minerals, and antioxidants. By improving your diet in this way you will achieve more stable blood sugar, greater hormonal balance, and better health.

What can I expect?

If you are overweight, these recipes can help you to gradually lose weight. How much and how fast depends on how overweight you are, how much you exercise, how much stress you experience, and, last but not least, your genes. You should not expect to lose more than 2 to 3 pounds of body fat per week, unless you are very overweight. If you lose more than this, it will affect your muscle mass, which is not good, as it is muscle that keeps the metabolism active.

If you often crave sweet or starchy foods, following the principles of this way of eating will help you regain control of what you eat.

If you are underweight, these recipes can help you reach a healthy weight.

If your body weight is normal, you will neither gain nor lose weight, but you may feel much better.

If you have high blood pressure, elevated cholesterol or high triglycerides, a balanced diet will improve your health and help you avoid cardiovascular disorders.

If you have diabetes, you will gain better control of your blood sugar; your cholesterol and triglyceride levels should decrease and your blood pressure should improve.

If you often feel tired and sluggish an hour or so after a meal, you may suffer from "reactive hypoglycemia," a symptom of low blood sugar. This can mean that you are insulin sensitive, and that your blood sugar drops a relatively short time after you have eaten highly refined foods such as white bread, processed cereals, and sugar. Incorporating the dishes in this book into your diet can prevent or greatly reduce such symptoms.

Allergies, inflammatory conditions like arthritis and asthma, chronic fatigue syndrome, fibromyalgia, and stress-related disorders often improve as a result of a change in eating habits. The typical modern diet, with its high intake of sugars and starches and low intake of omega-3 essential fatty acids, may contribute greatly to such problems, because it causes unstable blood sugar levels with accompanying hormonal turbulence. Again, the recipes that follow can help by stabilizing blood sugar levels and improving hormonal balance.

So this is far more than just a weight-loss diet. *Eating the Greek Way* can help keep your blood sugar stable throughout the day, keeping you mentally alert and physically fit. These recipes are designed to help you do everything you can to prevent lifestyle diseases such as type II diabetes, cardiovascular disease (heart attack, stroke, high blood pressure, and other diseases of the heart and arteries), joint problems and certain forms of cancer. They are suitable for the whole family, adults and children alike—remember that this is the way people around the Mediterranean have traditionally eaten and as a result they have enjoyed a level of good health that is the envy of most other Western nations. Most important, the whole family will truly enjoy these recipes that celebrate the happy marriage of delicious food and good health.

To learn more about how *Eating the Greek Way* works, read on, but if you want to skip to the recipes, they start on page 57.

The importance of balanced blood sugar

Balancing the blood sugar through diet is central to *Eating the Greek Way*—and the key to that is choosing the correct carbohydrates. Your body reacts to the food you eat by producing different hormones, and hormonal balance is essential to staying healthy. Two of the most important hormones are insulin and glucagon. Their main task is to regulate the body's blood sugar level. Every time you eat food that contains carbohydrates (like bread, potatoes, rice, pasta, sugar and to a lesser extent vegetables, fruit, and legumes) your blood sugar will rise. The pancreas reacts to this by producing insulin. The amount of insulin produced depends on the amount and type of carbohydrate that you eat: Carbohydrates that are rapidly absorbed and converted into blood sugar stimulate the release of a high level of insulin; carbohydrates that are absorbed and converted into blood sugar more slowly cause a less pronounced rise in blood sugar and a lower level of insulin in the blood.

One of the most important functions of insulin is to ensure that blood sugar is absorbed into the cells of the body. It is stored first in the liver and muscles, but if these stores are already full, insulin makes the body store the excess as fat, especially around the waist. Insulin is the energy- and fat-storing hormone of the body.

A high level of insulin in the blood makes it difficult, if not impossible, for the body to burn fat from its fat stores and therefore makes losing weight almost impossible. The same is true if the relationship between insulin and glucagon is unbalanced. Glucagon promotes the burning of body fat to provide energy, and when the body is producing glucagon (triggered by the consumption of protein), it is not producing insulin.

The more overweight you are, the more insulin there will be in your blood. The more insulin you have in your blood, the easier it will be to store fat and gain weight.

Besides making it almost impossible to lose weight, too much insulin can also result in long-term damage to your body. The more often your body experiences a high level of insulin, the more difficult it becomes for insulin to lower blood sugar.

Eating the Greek Way

To sum up, this means:

▶ "slow carbs"—vegetables, salads, legumes, whole grains —keep blood sugar stable

▶ protein—especially fish and shellfish, legumes, low-fat dairy food—maintains muscle and keeps metabolism active

▶ healthy fats—olive oil, nuts, seeds, oily fish—have many vital health-protective effects

(continued on page 15)

A typical day Eating the Greek Way

Breakfast

▶ 2 scrambled eggs, 1¾ ounces smoked salmon
▶ 1 or 2 grilled tomatoes drizzled with
  1 teaspoon olive oil

Snack

▶ ½ cup low-fat plain yogurt with 1 kiwi fruit and
  1 tablespoon ground flaxseed

Lunch

▶ 3–5½ ounces cooked chicken mixed with 1 cup
  cooked chickpeas
▶ mixed arugula and watercress salad with
  tomatoes and avocado
▶ 2 tablespoons homemade vinaigrette

Snack

(could be eaten after dinner, if dinner is early)
▶ 1 apple
▶ 10 to 12 peanuts

Dinner

▶ 1 cup Broccoli and Cauliflower Soup (page 61)
▶ 1 serving of Red Mullet with Orange, Ginger,
  and Cilantro Sauce (page 101)
▶ 7 ounces steamed mixed vegetables
▶ ½ cup cooked brown rice or couscous

Mastering stress

Stress is something everybody experiences at some time or other. To live in our modern society and be immune to stress is impossible. Each time you experience stress, be it "positive" or "negative," your body produces stress hormones. To secure the survival of the species all living creatures have developed protective mechanisms against danger. The "fight or flight" response allows us to get out of danger fast. Faced with potential danger your heart beats faster, your blood pressure goes up, you may start perspiring, and you feel very alert. All this was very helpful for ancient man, who lived in a dangerous environment. If he were faced with a predatory animal, for example, it allowed him to take decisive action and utilize the energy that the fight or flight response provides.

Modern stress, however, rarely has anything to do with real danger. If you experience this sort of stress reaction as a result of being stuck in a traffic jam, for example, you have no opportunity to "complete" the stress response by using up the energy the stress hormones provide. Experiencing this reaction on a regular basis leads to constantly elevated levels of the stress hormones, adrenalin and cortisol. This sort of chronic stress is one of the major causes of modern lifestyle disorders.

An unhealthy diet can also lead to stress. Why? Because stress hormones are secreted when the blood sugar is unstable, which occurs when you eat high-glycemic foods. If you eat a baguette or a piece of cake, you will have a sharp and sudden rise in blood sugar. This makes your body increase its production of insulin, which will make your blood sugar level drop about $1\frac{1}{2}$ hours after the meal. The brain, which is dependent on a stable blood sugar level, interprets the falling blood sugar as a danger signal. If your body doesn't intervene, your blood sugar will keep falling and you will pass out. Hence the body starts producing adrenalin and cortisol in order to stabilize the blood sugar at a normal level.

A combination of bad nutrition, lack of exercise, high work pace, poor quality of sleep, and lack of relaxation can lead to chronic stress. Chronic stress lowers the chromium level in your body, which leads to higher insulin levels and subsequently an irresistible craving for sweet or starchy food. A chronically elevated insulin level can trigger a wide range of symptoms, including overweight, diabetes, anxiety and depression, fibromyalgia, and chronic fatigue syndrome.

You can, however, do something about this. First you have to find the factors that cause you stress and avoid them wherever possible. This is not always easy. None of us is immune to stress, so learning to cope with it is as important as seeking to avoid and reduce it wherever possible. This can be achieved through a combination of stress management techniques (such as tai chi, yoga, and meditation) and physical exercise, together with a healthy, well-balanced, low-glycemic diet.

(continued from page 12)

The pancreas tries to compensate for this by secreting more insulin. The more rapidly-absorbed carbohydrates you consume, the more insulin your body will produce, and as a result you soon become caught in a vicious circle of hyperinsulinemia (higher insulin production) and reduced insulin sensitivity (insulin resistance). When this happens, your insulin level remains high constantly, whether you have eaten or not. However, it is only the blood-sugar-lowering effect of insulin that has deteriorated. Insulin still continues to promote fat storage. This will result in weight gain and a greater risk of developing type II diabetes, high cholesterol levels, high blood pressure, and cardiovascular disorders, as well as certain types of cancer.

How to choose "slow" carbs

Slow carbs (also known as "good" carbs) are carbohydrates that raise the blood sugar level slowly and therefore do not cause a surge in insulin. The easiest way to determine which carbs are "slow" is by looking at their Glycemic Index (GI), though as we will see, it does throw up a few anomalies. GI is a method of ranking carbohydrate foods according to their effect on blood sugar: The faster they are digested and absorbed by the small intestine, the faster and higher the rise in blood sugar, and the higher the GI. Pure glucose can be absorbed directly into the bloodstream, so it has an immediate effect on blood sugar: On a scale of 0 to 100, glucose has a GI of 100.

GI compares foods based on equal carbohydrate content, not equal amount of food: 50 g (1¾ ounces) of glucose is pure carbohydrate, whereas the GI for boiled carrot is based on the amount of boiled carrot that contains 50 g of carbs—667 g (about 1½ pounds). Most non-starchy vegetables have a very low carbohydrate content, usually less than 5 percent. You would therefore need to eat a very large amount of tomatoes or celery, for instance, in order to ingest the 50 g of carbohydrate needed to

measure their GI. For this reason, they do not have a GI rating.

Foods that do not contain carbohydrates do not have a direct influence on blood sugar; consequently their GI is zero. This is why there are no GI numbers for foods that consist primarily of protein, such as eggs, chicken, meat, and fish. The same is true of foods that consist mainly of fat, such as butter and oils.

Glycemic Load—taking GI a step further

It is tempting to take a Glycemic Index list and say that all food with a high GI is unhealthy and everything with a low GI is good for you. The truth is always more complicated. GI is by no means the only health measure. If it were, margarine, with a GI of 0, would be very healthy, but that is not the case (see Trans Fats, page 45). Furthermore, you cannot say that bananas and mangoes are bad for you, even though their GI is relatively high.

If we concentrate solely on what is good or bad for your blood sugar—ignoring vitamins, minerals, and fat for the moment—the amount of carbohydrates eaten is clearly important. However, the GI is a measure of how fast the carbohydrate in any given food raises blood sugar; it says nothing about the amount of carbohydrate in the food, i.e. how much of it you would need to eat to elicit the response suggested by its GI. Remember, the level of insulin produced is based on the amount of carbs as well as how fast they are converted to blood sugar.

Researchers from Harvard University have therefore come up with the Glycemic Load (GL). The GL is, in the same way as the GI, an index ranking foods according to their effect on blood sugar. However, while GI gives us information on how fast blood sugar rises after we eat 50 g (1¾ ounces) of digestible carbohydrate in various foods, the GL takes into account both the GI and the amount of carbohydrate in 100 g (3½ ounces) of food, or a given portion. It therefore gives a far more accurate assessment of foods, because it reflects the effect on the blood sugar of a specific portion of a food.

The GL principle means that a number of foods blacklisted under the GI system now appear in a more favorable light. Watermelon is a good example. It has a GI of 72 because the type of carbohydrate it contains was found to raise blood sugar rapidly. However, since it contains very little of that carbohydrate its GL per 100 g (3½ ounces) is only 4.

At the back of the book you will find a chart listing both the GI and GL of many common foods.

Protein

Protein is crucial to our bodies. Our cells, hormones, and immune system are based on and communicate through proteins, so we must ensure that we get enough of this vital nutrient. Proteins are made up of compounds called amino acids, of which there are about twenty different kinds. Eleven of these can be produced by the human body. The remaining nine cannot be produced in the body and must be provided by the food we eat. These are called "essential amino acids" and if we do not get enough of them our bodily functions will deteriorate.

There are two sources of protein: animal protein and plant protein. Animal protein is found in milk and other dairy products, eggs, all meats, poultry, fish, and shellfish. Note that it is the saturated fat in dairy products and meat that is less healthy in large quantities, not the protein. If you choose lean meats and low-fat dairy products, fat is not an issue. Plant protein is mainly found in nuts; legumes such as beans, lentils, and chickpeas; and, to a lesser extent, in vegetables. For guidelines on choosing healthy sources of protein, see pages 31–39.

It is absolutely essential that you eat enough protein. Too little protein can lead to loss of lean body mass, or muscle. Muscles, large and small, are important for movement and protecting our vital inner organs. The muscles also constitute the part of the body that burns the most energy; so less muscle mass means a slower metabolism. Many age-related illnesses are linked to the loss of muscle. Many protein foods are also a source of important vitamins and minerals, so a low intake may result in a lack of antioxidants produced by the body—and these are part of our defence against premature ageing and illness.

Protein's role in metabolism

Protein is a key element for an efficient metabolism, and our consumption of protein has an effect on a number of hormones. Most importantly, protein stimulates production of the growth hormone IGF-1 and the hormone glucagon. The growth hormone increases muscle mass, while glucagon promotes the burning of body fat to provide energy. Glucagon's main function is to increase blood sugar if it is falling (for instance, during fasting or between meals), thus ensuring a steady energy supply for the body. Blood sugar is released from the liver's sugar supply (glycogen) and is also produced from proteins and fat. When the body is producing glucagon the effect is less fat storage and more burning of body fat.

Let me emphasize that this is not a high-protein diet. The amount of protein I recommend (see page 21) is somewhat higher than most of us are used to (at the expense of carbohydrates), but the total amount is not high.

Fats

Nothing is as important to our health as eating the right kind of fat. The low rates of heart disease and other such conditions in those eating a traditional Mediterranean diet, where olive oil plays a central role, is testament to that. So, as with carbohydrates and protein, the key is to choose your source wisely.

In food, fat is found in the form of triglycerides. When digested, these triglycerides are split into

their components: glycerol and three fatty acids. Nature contains numerous fatty acids, but only some play an important role in nutrition.

A number of fatty acids are important because they are building blocks for substances that are part of our immune system and have a positive influence on inflammatory reactions. Others are vital to a well-functioning metabolism, because we need the right kind of fat from our food in order to burn fat. Obese individuals often lack enough essential fatty acids, or the relationship between the types of fat they eat is wrong, and they have too much stored saturated fat (either originating directly from the diet or converted from excess carbohydrate). In combination with antioxidants, essential fatty acids influence our defense mechanisms against cancer, while others are important in preventing illnesses such as diabetes and heart disease.

All fats contain both saturated and unsaturated fatty acids but are usually described as saturated or unsaturated depending on the proportions of fatty acids present. Butter, for instance, is usually thought of as a saturated fat because it contains 60 to 65 percent saturated and 30 to 35 percent unsaturated fat. Within the unsaturated category are two types of fats: monounsaturated and polyunsaturated. The human body is able to produce saturated and monounsaturated fatty acids but not some types of polyunsaturated fatty acids. Some of these, however, are essential for good health; the only way we can obtain these is through our diet. These are called essential fatty acids, usually referred to as omega-3 and omega-6. These fatty acids are an integral part of all cell membranes. The brain and nervous system consist mainly of these essential fatty acids, and depression and many disorders of the nervous system are linked to a low intake of omega-3 fatty acids. Western diets are generally too high in omega-6 and too low in omega-3 and this imbalance promotes chronic inflammation, which is the cause of many painful and life-threatening disorders.

You will find more guidance on fats in the section on "Ingredients for good health"(see pages 44–45).

Exercise for better health

Eating the Greek Way is not just about what you eat. Exercise is essential for good health and a combination of eating the right foods, regular exercise, and a healthier lifestyle in general will give you the best results, whether your aim is to lose weight or simply stay as healthy as you possibly can.

Many people believe that you need to do strenuous exercise if you want to lose weight and be in good health. This is not correct. Without a change in diet, the weight loss that will result from exercise alone is small. Moreover, it is not necessary to train very hard to gain positive health effects. The crucial thing is to turn a form of exercise that you enjoy into a part of your everyday life: You don't have to "spin" yourself to death on an exercise bike. It is better to exercise moderately, but daily. Walking for at least 20 to 30 minutes every day and strength-training the major muscle groups (especially the thighs) 2 to 3 times a week is adequate for many people, when combined with a healthy diet.

Human beings are designed to move in order to get food. During the Stone Age we would have walked an average of 18 miles a day to find food—sometimes unsuccessfully. If we got something to eat, the important thing was to stay put and not use energy unnecessarily—until we got hungry again. This is the reason why it makes sense to exercise early in the day and on an empty stomach. It goes well with our hormones and biorhythms. When we get up in the morning, the carbohydrate store in the liver is nearly empty, the blood pressure is relatively low, and the insulin level is at its lowest. Low insulin means that the body can more easily burn stored fat as fuel. Remember that a high level of insulin means fat storage whereas low insulin means that fat can be burnt efficiently.

If you can't get up early enough to fit in a session, try finding ways of exercising on your way to work. Perhaps you could walk or cycle to work. Or you could get off the bus a couple of stops earlier and get a brisk 20- to 30-minute walk. Exercising early in the day every day is simply the best gift you can give yourself and your metabolism. That said, any exercise, irrespective of the time of day you do it, is clearly better than none at all. In fact, being physically inactive is a much greater health hazard than being overweight. You can be "fit fat" and reduce the risk of most diseases by exercising on a regular basis. Sadly, being both physically inactive and overweight is not uncommon, and this increases your health risks even more.

What should I eat before and after exercising?

Avoid carbohydrates, especially high-glycemic foods, before you exercise as this increases the levels of blood sugar and insulin and decreases fat burning. However, after tough (not moderate) exercise eating high-glycemic food will help you recover more quickly.

Remember that you will get the most out of exercising if you provide your body with an appropriate amount of protein. Exercise stimulates the production of growth hormones that build more muscle, but only if there are enough "bricks," i.e. proteins. Ideally, you should drink a large glass of water and have some low-glycemic fruit as soon as you get up and then exercise for 20 to 30 minutes. To maximize the effect of morning exercise, especially weight training, have 15 to 20 g (½ to ¾ ounce) of protein (the amount found in a serving of yogurt or cottage cheese) shortly before starting the exercise or no later than 1 to 1½ hours afterwards. This increases the production of glucagon and growth hormone, thereby enhancing muscle tissue and fat burning. After exercising, you should eat a well-balanced breakfast, treating it as a main meal (see next page).

Basic principles of Eating the Greek Way

Technically I call Eating the Greek Way the isoglycemic diet (*isos* is the Greek word for "equal"): It is all about balance. The aim is to restore a more natural balance of the types of carbohydrates, proteins, and fats you eat.

You will be eating fewer refined and processed foods and a greater range of natural foods—those that suit you genetically and that will improve your metabolism. Nothing is banned (I'm just being realistic), but if you eat less favorable carbs and fats, do so in moderation and balance their effect with a greater intake of healthy carbs and proteins.

Approximately one-third of your total energy intake (by which I mean calories, not amount of food) should come from low- and medium-glycemic carbohydrates: These are carbohydrates that don't make your blood sugar rise rapidly. Less than one-third should come from high-quality animal and plant proteins, and the rest from minimally processed natural fat, primarily monounsaturated and

polyunsaturated fats, but also, to a lesser degree, saturated fats. Sounds too much like science? Don't worry, you will not need to count grams, percentages, or calories. In fact, you will not need to count or weigh anything at all; the palm of your hand is all you need to judge the amount of food you should eat, as I'll explain shortly.

Most of your meals should consist of approximately one-third protein foods and two-thirds low-glycemic carbohydrates. One meal a day—your "reward" meal—may consist of one-third protein, half low-glycemic carbohydrates and one-sixth medium- or high-glycemic carbohydrates. You can choose whether to have this for breakfast, lunch, or dinner. To be in tune with human metabolic biorhythm, it is probably best to have your reward meal as your breakfast or lunch, but many people will choose dinner, for practical and social reasons.

Fat does not get its own allotment as it is needed in smaller amounts. It is often "hidden" as part of

	Saturated fat: Butter, cheese	
High GL	Sugar, white bread, white flour, potatoes	
GL-regulating	Unsaturated fat: Extra-virgin olive oil, avocado oil, nuts and seeds, oily fish	
Medium–high GL	Durum wheat pasta, non-sticky rice, e.g. basmati, long-grain, whole-grain products, dense bread made from less processed grains	
GL-regulating	Protein: Fish, chicken, lean meat, game, eggs, yogurt, cottage cheese	
Low GL	Vegetables, legumes, low-glycemic fruit	

The Eating the Greek Way food triangle

A simple way to visualize this way of eating is to use a food triangle. As you can see, the base of the triangle consists of vegetables and legumes with a low GL. Fruit with a low GL also comes into this category. These foods (see pages 39—40) make up the main part of all your meals.

Higher up, you will find GL-regulating foods rich in protein and unsaturated fat. These make up about one-third of every meal.

Near the top are medium- to high-glycemic carbohydrates (mainly starchy and sweet foods). Small helpings of these may be eaten once a day in your reward meal.

food preparation or in sauces or salad dressings. The best fats are the unsaturated types found in extra-virgin olive oil, nuts, cold-pressed nut oils, avocados, oily fish, and flaxseed oil. Limit your intake of saturated fat (mainly found in animal sources such as butter, cheese, and meat).

Water is the best "health drink": 8 cups is a minimum for most adults. A glass of wine with a meal is fine in terms of health—but if you are trying to lose weight I would recommend that you avoid alcohol or drink it as part of a reward meal.

You may eat almost as much as you want until you feel comfortably full (do not eat too quickly as it takes 10 to 15 minutes for satiety signals to reach the brain), but you must always balance what you eat. If you want a second helping, that's fine, but don't just eat more carbohydrates. You should eat a corresponding (smaller) amount of protein. No meal or snack should be without protein.

How much should I eat?

Without weighing and measuring, there is an easy way to envisage what your meals should look like. For an adult, the amount of protein food should be about as big and thick as the palm of your hand. Palm size varies from one person to another and is proportionate with the rest of the body. This is the amount of protein-based food (cooked and ready to eat) that you need at each of your three main meals per day.

A serving of vegetables and legumes as well as low-glycemic fruits and berries should be twice as big as the protein part: two palms.

For a reward meal, reduce the vegetables, legumes, and low-glycemic fruits to one and a half palms. Enjoy up to half a palm of bread, pasta, rice, dessert, cheese, or wine.

Snacks should be about half to one-third the size of main meals, keeping otherwise to the proportions.

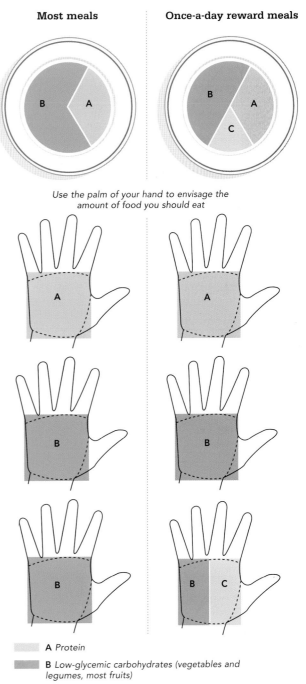

Most meals | **Once-a-day reward meals**

Use the palm of your hand to envisage the amount of food you should eat

A Protein

B Low-glycemic carbohydrates (vegetables and legumes, most fruits)

C Medium- and high-glycemic carbohydrates (such as bread, potatoes, pasta, rice, grain products, dessert, cheese or wine)

What can I eat?

Legumes

1 to 3 servings per day
1 serving = 1cup

▶ beans
▶ chickpeas
▶ dried peas
▶ lentils

Vegetables

Unlimited amount
▶ artichokes
▶ asparagus
▶ bamboo shoots
▶ bell peppers
▶ bean sprouts
▶ bok choy
▶ broccoli
▶ Brussels sprouts
▶ cabbage, all kinds
▶ cauliflower
▶ celery
▶ cucumber
▶ eggplant
▶ fennel
▶ green beans
▶ green peas
▶ leeks
▶ onions, garlic
▶ radishes
▶ salad greens
   (e.g. lettuce, chicory, arugula)
▶ scallions
▶ spinach
▶ tomatoes
▶ watercress
▶ zucchini

Fruit

2 servings per day
1 serving = 1 whole fruit unless otherwise indicated or $3\frac{1}{2}$ ounces berries, cherries, or grapes

▶ apple
▶ apricots (3)
▶ berries, all kinds
▶ cherries
▶ grapefruit
▶ grapes
▶ kiwi fruit (1–2)
▶ melon
▶ nectarine
▶ orange
▶ peach
▶ pear
▶ plum
▶ pomegranate
▶ passion fruit (2)
▶ tangerines (2)
▶ watermelon (up to 7-ounce serving)

Protein sources

3 to 5 servings per day, of which at least 1 serving is fish
1 serving = 3–7 ounces prepared;
approximately 4–6 ounces raw

▶ eggs (1 serving = 2–3 whole eggs or 5 whites)
▶ fish (preferably oily fish), shellfish
▶ chicken breast, turkey breast
▶ game (venison, rabbit, pheasant, etc.)
▶ lean meat from lamb, beef or pork
▶ cottage cheese (5–6 tablespoons)
▶ tofu ($3\frac{1}{2}$-ounce serving)

Root vegetables

1 to 2 servings per day
1 serving = 3½ ounces boiled, 7 ounces raw

▶ beets
▶ carrots
▶ celery root
▶ Jerusalem artichokes
▶ sweet potato

Fat sources

1 to 3 tbs per day, divided among all meals

▶ extra-virgin olive oil or canola oil
▶ sesame oil
▶ homemade mayonnaise made with extra-virgin olive oil
▶ half an avocado

Nuts and seeds

1 to 3 servings per day
1 serving = 2 tablespoons

▶ 10–12 almonds, cashew nuts, peanuts, or hazelnuts
▶ 6–8 walnut halves
▶ 4 macadamia nuts
▶ 2 Brazil nuts
▶ sesame, sunflower, pumpkin, or flax seeds

Dairy products

1 serving per day

▶ 5–6 tablespoons fat-free or low-fat plain yogurt
▶ 1 cup skim or low-fat milk
▶ 1 cup soy milk

Coarse grain products

1 serving per day
1 serving = ½ cup boiled grains, 3 tablespoons cereal, or 1 slice of wholegrain bread

▶ brown basmati rice
▶ wild rice
▶ oats
▶ barley
▶ couscous
▶ quinoa
▶ roasted buckwheat kernels (kasha)
▶ high-fiber, whole-grain cereal or unsweetened muesli (preferably without dried fruit)
▶ whole-wheat or protein-enriched/low-carb pasta
▶ very dark whole-grain bread

Taste enhancers

Unlimited amount

▶ Dijon mustard
▶ vinegar (all kinds)
▶ herbs
▶ spices
▶ chile peppers
▶ Tabasco and other hot-pepper sauces
▶ lemon and lime juice
▶ grated fresh horseradish

Beverages

Unlimited amount

▶ water (at least 8 cups a day)
▶ decaffeinated coffee or decaffeinated tea
▶ green tea

Sample weekly menus

This two-week menu plan provides an example of how Eating the Greek Way might work in practice. Its purpose is to provide inspiration to help you get started on a new way of eating. There is no need to follow it strictly; rather, think of it as a guide to help you break away from your current eating habits and choose the path to good health. All of us have different daily routines so you will undoubtedly need to adapt these meal suggestions to your circumstances: If, for example, you work in an office with no facilities to heat food for lunch then you can still enjoy the convenience of a soup that you have made in advance, but you will need to heat it up before you leave home and put it in a thermos flask. In contrast, if you work from home you will be able to enjoy many more freshly-cooked hot meals at lunchtime.

Please note that the times indicated for each meal are there to make sure that you eat often enough. Obviously you may adjust them to suit your own schedule.

It can be difficult to change food habits on your own, so it is important that you seek support from those close to you. It is also vital—if you do not do the shopping or cooking—that the person preparing food at home is willing to help you. Besides, a healthy diet is good for the whole family!

The following tips should help you either adapt these menu plans to your needs, or devise your own, while still fulfilling the general guidelines of the diet.

► Cooking food in advance is a great way to save time and effort. Whenever you cook a meal that can be chilled or frozen, make extra portions and freeze or store for later use—either as a lunch, or a main course on nights when you don't have the time or inclination to cook. I cannot overestimate the value of coming home after a long day and being able to enjoy a healthy, homemade meal

that requires no effort. The menus on the following pages include a number of soups and main courses that can be prepared in advance—these are indicated by an asterisk.

► The suggested amounts are meant only as a guideline. Feel free to increase them if necessary, so that you feel pleasantly full, but make sure that each meal is properly balanced.

► Variety is vital. Mindlessly eating the same foods day after day is a sure path to weight gain, and diets that restrict your choice of foods are difficult to stick to for very long. But there's more to it than that. Many vitamins and minerals work best in combination with other micronutrients, and eating a variety of foods will ensure you get a good mix of micronutrients.

► Make sure that you have some protein-rich food (fish, poultry, egg, milk, cottage cheese, yogurt, tofu) with every meal and snack, in order to obtain the best possible glycemic effect.

► Cottage cheese, fromage blanc, and quark are all good, low-fat sources of protein. For variety, add fresh berries, chopped nuts, spices, or fresh herbs.

► Plain, unsweetened yogurt is another good source of protein. If you're trying to lose weight, look for fat-free yogurt—it tastes just as good as the regular type. Avoid fruit-flavored yogurts, as most are loaded with sugar. Opt for sugar-free alternatives, if available.

► A squeeze of fresh lemon juice over cooked vegetables, salads, fish, and shellfish, and even some poultry and meat dishes, reduces the glycemic effect and adds a wonderful fresh taste of the Mediterranean.

► Many meals and snacks benefit from the addition of 1 to 2 teaspoons of flaxseed oil just before you eat them: This gives you the benefits of omega-3 fats and reduces the glycemic effect of your meal.

Possible menu week 1

	7am Breakfast	10am Snack
Monday	Small bowl of unsweetened muesli 1 tablespoon ground flaxseed 1 cup skim milk 1 cup fresh berries	4–5 ounces cottage cheese 1 tablespoon pumpkin seeds
Tuesday	2 scrambled eggs Mushrooms cooked with 1 teaspoon olive oil	½ cup plain yogurt 1 cup fresh berries
Wednesday	Small bowl of mixed fruit salad ½ cup plain yogurt 2 tablespoons mixed chopped nuts	4–5 ounces cottage cheese 3 ounces cooked shrimp dill
Thursday	2 boiled eggs 1 slice soy and linseed bread 1–2 tablespoons cottage cheese 1 peach or nectarine	1 apple 10 almonds
Friday	Small bowl of porridge 1 tablespoon ground flaxseed 1 grated apple	½ cup plain yogurt 1–2 tablespoons sunflower or pumpkin seeds 1 pear
Saturday	½ small orange-fleshed melon 1 slice pumpernickel bread 2–3 tablespoons cottage cheese 5 ounces cooked shrimp	1 kiwi fruit 10 hazelnuts
Sunday	½–1 grapefruit 2 eggs (cooked in 1 teaspoon olive oil) 4–5 ounces smoked mackerel 1–2 tomatoes, grilled	1 apple 2 Brazil nuts

* indicates that the dish is a "make ahead" recipe

12.30pm Lunch	4pm Snack	7pm Dinner
4–7 ounces grilled chicken or turkey breast Mixed leaf salad with artichoke hearts, olives, and 1 tablespoon freshly grated Parmesan cheese	1 pear 10 almonds	Hummus (page 87) and raw vegetables *Salmon Fishcakes (page 94) Stir-fried green vegetables
4–5 ounces smoked mackerel Arugula and avocado salad 1 slice pumpernickel bread	⅔ cup grapes 2 Brazil nuts	Chicken, Walnut, and Red Bean Salad (page 77)
*Greek Vegetable Soup (page 60)	2–3 teaspoons unsweetened peanut butter Celery stalks	Grilled trout Avocado, Zucchini, and Pasta Salad (page 80) Green salad
Canned sardines in olive oil mixed with chopped red bell pepper, celery, scallions, lemon juice, and 1 teaspoon mayonnaise, on crisp lettuce	½ cup plain yogurt 4 walnut halves 1–1¼ ounces bittersweet chocolate (70 % cacao)	4–7 ounces cold ham or turkey Tomato Salad with Beans and Basil (page 77) Watercress salad
*Marinated Shrimp (page 94) mixed green salad	4–5 ounces cottage cheese 4 cherry tomatoes fresh basil	*Chickpea Fritters (page 137) Greek Salad (page 82)
Mussels with White Beans and Olives (page 89) Steamed green beans	Eggplant Purée (page 85) Raw carrot and red bell pepper	*Stuffed Peppers (page 122) Green salad with vinaigrette Raspberry Yogurt Sorbet (page 150)
*Mushroom Soup with Goat Cheese (page 64)	8 olives 10 almonds	*Pork Casserole with Chickpeas and Orange (page 120) ⅔ cup cooked couscous Steamed broccoli and snow peas

Possible menu week 2

	7am Breakfast	10am Snack
Monday	3 tablespoons All-Bran 1 tablespoon ground flaxseed 1 cup skim milk ½–1 grapefruit	4–5 ounces cottage cheese Chopped red bell pepper, carrot, and zucchini
Tuesday	2 scrambled eggs 2 ounces smoked salmon Cherry tomatoes 1 kiwi fruit	1 apple 2 Brazil nuts
Wednesday	Small bowl of mixed fruit salad ½ cup plain yogurt 2 tablespoon chopped nuts	Grated carrot 1 tablespoon sunflower or sesame seeds 1 teaspoon olive oil or sesame oil
Thursday	3 tablespoons unsweetened muesli 1 tablespoon sunflower seeds 1 cup skim milk 1 cup fresh berries	2–3 teaspoons unsweetened peanut butter Celery stalks
Friday	3 slices of ham 2 poached eggs Grilled mushrooms	⅔ cup grapes 2 Brazil nuts
Saturday	Small bowl of porridge 1 tablespoon ground flaxseed 1 kiwi fruit ½ cup plain yogurt	4–5 ounces cottage cheese 1 cup fresh berries
Sunday	2 eggs cooked with 1 teaspoon olive oil 2 slices of lean bacon 1–2 tomatoes, grilled	1 pear 6–8 walnut halves

12.30pm Lunch	4pm Snack	7pm Dinner
*Pork Casserole with Chickpeas and Orange (page 120)	⅔ cup grapes 10 almonds	*Lemon-Marinated Sardines (page 96) Watercress, tomato, and avocado salad
*Mushroom Soup with Goat Cheese (page 64)	2–3 teaspoons unsweetened peanut butter Carrot sticks	Chicken Kebabs with Fresh Herbs (page 109) Basmati Rice with Nuts (page 145) Tomato Salad with Beans and Basil (page 77) Green salad
Tuna, Chickpea, and Avocado Salad (page 74)	4–5 ounces cottage cheese 4 cherry tomatoes	Meat mixture from *Stuffed Peppers (page 122) ⅔ cup cooked pasta Steamed mixed vegetables
5 ounces cooked shrimp mixed with 1 tablespoon fromage blanc, 1 teaspoon tomato paste, lemon juice, and cilantro Watercress salad	1 orange 4 macadamia nuts	4–7 ounces grilled chicken or turkey breast Black Beans with Herbs (page 141) Zucchini and Mushroom Gratin (page 129)
Mung Bean and Tomato Salad (page 142) 1 orange	2–3 tablespoons hummus Raw cauliflower, carrot, and red bell pepper	Swordfish with Garlic and Walnut Sauce (page 98) Steamed green beans ½ cup cooked brown rice
*Salmon Fish Cakes (page 94) Green salad with avocado	8 olives 10 almonds	Zucchini and Fennel Omelet (page 131) Puy Lentils with Red Wine (page 141)
*White Beans with Tomatoes (page 140) 5 ounces medium shrimp, grilled	Tzatziki (page 87) Carrot and celery	*Lamb with Apricots and Almonds (page 118) Herbed Quinoa Pilaf (page 144) Steamed spinach Baked Apples with Vanilla Sauce (page 154)

Ingredients for
good health

This chapter looks at the various foods that help optimize health—deliciously. There are more than 100 trillion cells in the human body, and in each cell there are thousands of biochemical reactions every second, every day throughout our lives. Food is involved in all of these reactions. Unfortunately, today's highly processed food rarely supplies us with everything we need to be truly healthy. It provides the energy to survive and function on a day-to-day basis, but it leaves a lot to be desired if we want optimum flavor, health, and vitality. Much of the food we eat consists of empty, useless calories, with ingredients that have been processed beyond recognition.

Our vitality and our ability to maintain or restore good health are totally dependent on our lifestyle and diet. You need food that satisfies and gives you nourishment, not just energy. But food should also nourish you in another way—it should be a positive and enjoyable aspect of your life, something to look forward to, something that will boost your family and social life. Food should be exciting and creative. The healthy, delicious ingredients and recipes in this book will ensure that eating well becomes a natural part of your life.

In the previous section I provided some guidance on what you should eat. Here, I'll look at those foods in more detail, starting with protein, such as fish, poultry, meat, game, eggs, and dairy products.

Protein

Protein is very important because, by stimulating the production of the metabolism-boosting hormone glucagon, it regulates the production of insulin. The effect of this is to stabilize blood sugar. Protein will generally lower the glycemic effect of a meal, which is important for everybody who wishes to have stable blood sugar, and particularly for those who are overweight or diabetic.

Most people get the bulk of the protein they

need from eating fish and shellfish, chicken and other poultry, various types of meat, eggs, dairy products, nuts, and also legumes, especially soybean products. Protein is made up of 20 amino acids, nine of which cannot be produced in the body and need to be provided by our diet. However, all protein foods are not created equal: They contain varying amounts of these amino acids. The best composition of amino acids for the human body comes from animal sources such as meat, fish, poultry, and eggs.

Many vegetables and grains also contain protein, but vegetable sources of protein are generally lacking in one or more amino acids, so in order to obtain the full complement of protein from these sources, it is necessary to combine incomplete sources of protein, for instance legumes and grains. Soybeans are an exception as they provide a full and well-balanced mixture of essential amino acids—and are therefore a valuable and healthy protein for vegetarians and meat eaters alike. Spirulina (a type of algae) is another good protein source from the plant world.

Those who eat seafood and meat have a far greater choice of proteins—but some are healthier than others.

Fish and shellfish

If you are searching for a source of healthy protein, start with fish and shellfish. They contain a multitude of vitamins and minerals, especially B-vitamins and minerals such as selenium, iodine, zinc, phosphorus, and copper. Iodine is very important to the body's production of the hormone thyroxin, which influences metabolism. Shellfish is a particularly good source of zinc and selenium. Oysters are perhaps nature's best source of zinc, a mineral that is crucial for cell growth and repair, a strong immune system, brain function, eyesight, and reproduction (sperm motility as well as potency).

Fatty fish such as salmon, trout, mackerel,

sardines, and tuna contain essential omega-3 fatty acids and are at the same time a good source of the fat-soluble vitamins A, D, and E. The hugely beneficial omega-3 fatty acids lower triglycerides (fatty substances in the blood) and enhance insulin sensitivity, resulting in lower insulin levels in the blood and less insulin resistance. Both these effects lead to lower blood pressure and help to prevent heart disease. Omega-3 fatty acids also have a series of other health benefits, both because they form part of the structure of all our body's cells and because they contribute to the production of favorable anti-inflammatory substances.

How often should you eat fish and shellfish? As often as you can, but at least twice a week, especially oily fish. The only proviso is that you limit your intake of the larger oily fish such as tuna and swordfish, due to concerns about the toxins they may contain. These large fish eat smaller fish and live longer, so they are more likely to accumulate toxins such as mercury; smaller fish such as sardines are less likely to be contaminated to the same extent. Pregnant women are advised to avoid shark, marlin and swordfish and limit their intake of fresh and canned tuna. I advise pregnant women to eat plenty of white fish and to get their omega-3 fatty acids from high-quality supplements.

Vary your choice of fish—and don't forget shellfish. Shrimp, langoustines, scallops, squid, mussels, and clams taste delicious and are quick to cook. At one time some shellfish were thought to raise cholesterol levels but scientists have now rejected this theory.

Canned seafood is another healthy choice; and it is convenient and good value. Opt for varieties canned in olive oil or spring water—but avoid those canned in sunflower or other vegetable oil.

Chicken and other poultry

One of the great advantages of poultry, regardless of type, is that most of the fat, between 50 and 85 percent, is in the skin. The meat itself is fairly lean. By removing the skin you will get lean protein of very high quality. Poultry contains plenty of B-vitamins and is also rich in zinc, magnesium, and iron. The darker parts, such as the legs, contain more iron than the lighter parts, which on the other hand are quite rich in magnesium. And did you know that duck contains more iron than beef?

The leanest poultry is turkey. Its low fat content means it is very important to use low temperatures when you cook whole turkey or turkey parts. By doing so you will retain the natural juices in the meat, and the result will be a succulent dish with no need for rich sauces to compensate for dry meat. Both chicken and turkey can be purchased ground to form the basis of a wide variety of low-fat dishes.

Pork, veal, bacon, and ham

Pork and veal are good sources of protein—as long as you choose lean cuts, such as fillet (tenderloin), medallions, or escalopes, and trim off any visible fat. Both meats have excellent nutritional profiles. They contain considerable amounts of minerals such as potassium, zinc, and phosphorous. Pork is particularly rich in vitamins B1 (thiamin), B12, and iron (iron from meat is absorbed by the body five times more efficiently than iron from plant sources); veal is a good source of the B-group vitamins and folic acid.

Fat enhances the flavor of meat and prevents it from becoming dry when it is cooked, so it is important to compensate for this when you prepare lean cuts of veal or pork. Marinating in olive oil and lemon juice—with garlic and herbs if you like—will give a very tasty and juicy result. You can also choose to fry the meat in olive oil at a low temperature.

If you like bacon, buy lean back bacon rather than streaky, trim off the fat before cooking, and enjoy it as an occasional treat rather than every day. Lean ham is a tasty addition to salads and any fat can easily be trimmed off.

Beef and lamb

These red meats are not a regular feature of the traditional healthy Mediterranean diet. They were mainly served on special occasions—and certainly not eaten three or four times a week, as many people now seem to do. But why has red meat, such as beef and lamb, acquired such a bad reputation from the point of view of health?

It is the saturated fat content that originally sparked off concerns. An excess of saturated fat in the diet, combined with a lack of exercise, contributes to a higher level of LDL cholesterol (the "bad" form of cholesterol) in the blood. As LDL cholesterol passes through the arteries it can become trapped in lesions on the artery walls, creating a fatty plaque. Here, the cholesterol is prone to damage (oxidation). Smoking, stress, a low intake of antioxidants (found mainly in vegetables, nuts, legumes, fruits, and berries) and a high intake of high-glycemic carbohydrates have all been shown to increase oxidation in the body. An elevated cholesterol level by itself is probably not enough to make you predisposed to heart problems. It is when the LDL cholesterol is oxidized that it can lead to heart disease. The trans fatty acids in hydrogenated fats (found in margarines and in many ready-made foods, from breakfast cereals and soups to cakes, cookies, pies, and other pastry products) have a much more harmful effect than saturated fat.

OK, so red meat is not the worst thing you can eat by any means. However, aside from its saturated fat content, there is another reason not to eat it too often. The saturated fat in red meat (and also in egg yolks) contains arachidonic acid, an omega-6 fatty acid. An excess of this fatty acid causes the formation of inflammatory substances that can lead to high blood pressure, an increased tendency to blood coagulation and risk of thrombosis, as well as various inflammatory conditions such as chronic fatigue, arthritis, and flaky skin.

Is there anything positive to be said for red meat?

Of course there is. It tastes fantastic and contains protein of excellent quality, along with B-vitamins and important minerals such as iron and zinc. Personally, I do not eat red meat often, because I prefer fish, chicken, and turkey. That does not mean I never eat red meat. When I do, I choose the best and leanest parts, such as fillet of beef or leg of lamb.

When using ground meat, I always pick a good piece of meat with no fat and ask the butcher to grind it for me. You can also do this quite easily yourself, using a food processor. This way you will be sure that the meat is lean. Pre-packed ground meat can contain quite a lot of fat (and ice water that you pay a high price for).

One red meat you may not have considered is ostrich. It is very tasty, tender, and extremely lean. It has a taste somewhere between beef and lamb and is as lean as venison. It is now being farmed more widely so it is becoming more easily available.

Game

Game is some of the healthiest meat you can eat. It is low in fat and high in iron, and if you buy a wild specimen, as opposed to farmed game, it will have had a significantly better diet and way of life than most chickens, cows, and pigs.

The fat also contains a somewhat higher level of omega-3 fatty acids than regular red meat.

Now that venison is farmed it has become more popular and widely available. Hare and wild rabbit are also good choices, though they are not always readily available. Game birds such as pheasant, partridge, and wild duck are also a good choice of protein. Young birds can be roasted in no time but older birds are somewhat tougher and need to be roasted slowly or cooked in a casserole.

Eggs

All eggs are a valuable source of protein, and eggs from poultry that live in a free and natural way are a rich source of other nutrients, including vitamin B12. Just like other animals, what the hens have been allowed to eat will influence the nutritional content of the eggs. This is especially true of the fat quality. If the hens do not get favorable omega-3 fatty acids through their natural diet, there will be little of it in the egg yolk. When buying eggs, try to find free-range eggs from a local farm; these are also sold in some supermarkets.

At one time there were health concerns about the cholesterol content of eggs. However, several studies have now established that eating eggs has no bearing on the level of cholesterol in the blood. As I mentioned above, eggs, like beef, do contain arachidonic acid, a fatty acid that can cause health problems if the level in the blood gets too high or for those who are sensitive to it. The major symptoms of sensitivity to, or an elevated level of, arachidonic acid are chronic exhaustion, poor sleep quality, problems getting out of bed in the morning, thin or fine hair, thin nails, indigestion, dry flaky skin, and rashes.

Dairy products

Dairy products, though not essential for good health, are a source of high-quality protein and several important vitamins and minerals, including B-vitamins and calcium. Unfortunately, some dairy foods are also high in saturated fat. Your best choices of dairy proteins are plain, unsweetened yogurt and cottage cheese. Fromage blanc and quark are alternatives to cottage cheese: All are low in saturated fat, but choose natural products, not sweetened, fruit-flavored versions.

On the whole, you should avoid high-fat cheeses, though I do not recommend that you eat processed reduced-fat cheeses instead. If you are a cheese-lover, enjoy an occasional piece of high-fat cheese as a treat, and serve it with fruit or salad, not with high-glycemic carbohydrates. A lot of cheese in combination with bread, crackers, or on pizza is one of the reasons many people are overweight. I use small amounts of feta cheese and Parmesan in salads and cooked vegetable dishes: With these strongly flavored cheeses, a little goes a long way.

I am not a great fan of milk—it contains a significant amount of the sugar lactose and, being a liquid, does not offer the same level of satiety as solid dairy foods. If you like milk, choose skim milk or low-fat, or try soy milk, which is a good alternative to dairy milk.

Nuts and seeds

You may not think of eating these very often, but nuts and seeds are a highly nutritious and natural food for humans. As well as protein they provide healthy fat and a range of vitamins and minerals, especially zinc, calcium, and magnesium. Almonds, cashews, and peanuts are highest in protein (they consist of about 20 percent protein, which is comparable to fish, poultry, and meat), followed by Brazil nuts, hazelnuts, pine nuts, and walnuts.

Fresh raw nuts and seeds are the best option. Roasted and salted nuts have usually been processed at a high temperature, so the fat they contain is not so healthy—and they often contain excess salt. Nuts and seeds make great snacks, on their own or with fruit or yogurt. Add them to salads or breakfast cereals or bake them in bread. And don't forget peanut butter; many shops now also sell cashew, almond, and other nut butters. Look for natural ones that don't have any additives.

Soybeans

These have the highest protein content of any beans—hence their inclusion here rather than with legumes in the "low-glycemic carbohydrates" section. Soybeans and soy protein products such as tofu contain isoflavones, substances that appear to lower LDL cholesterol. They also protect against oxidation, a process many believe to be more implicated in heart disease than the level of LDL cholesterol.

You can now often find soybeans in supermarkets, sold as edamame, which are young soybeans. They can be found both in their pods and shelled. Products made from soybeans are also easy to find: Try tofu, tempeh, and soy milk rather than any of the more highly processed "mock meat" foods.

Protein-rich pasta and bars

You can now buy protein-rich dry pasta with as much as 50 percent protein (regular pasta has around 10 percent). Pasta with a very high proportion of protein has a rubbery texture, but some brands that contain 25 to 30 percent protein can taste almost identical to regular pasta. It is usually enriched with soy protein and it has a lower GL than regular pasta, so it is especially suitable for people who are overweight or have diabetes.

Protein bars are becoming more readily available and can be a useful standby for people who don't have time to put together a protein-rich snack or small meal. The best of these are rather expensive because they contain the same amount of protein as one chicken breast, a wide range of vitamins and minerals, and very little carbohydrate and fat. They are not meant to be eaten every day. Look for ones without additives.

Low-glycemic carbohydrates

These make up the two-palm part of your plate, as described on page 21. Low-glycemic carbohydrates are mainly vegetables, legumes (which are also a good source of protein), and low-GL fruit (some fruits have a medium GL).

As you are by now aware, the carbohydrates in food stimulate the secretion of insulin to varying degrees. Eating the Greek Way is designed to keep the production of insulin low, thus keeping blood sugar stable. The result is a lower average insulin level and increased fat burning. This is not achieved by cutting out carbohydrates—which is not good

for health—but by ensuring that the majority of the carbohydrates you eat are low-glycemic carbs that raise blood sugar slowly and thus do not over-stimulate insulin secretion.

As a rule of thumb, the less physically active, the more overweight or insulin-resistant you are, the less carbohydrate you should eat. That said, it is difficult to get too much carbohydrate from eating vegetables, legumes, and low-GL fruit. However, it is all too easy when you eat sugar and other high-GL foods such as bread, potatoes, pasta, rice, and flour products. If you are overweight, you need to eat less sugar and starch and more vegetables and legumes.

Vegetables

Vegetables are crucial to good health and an aid to weight reduction. Because of the soluble fiber in vegetables, the carbohydrates are absorbed slowly, providing a gradual conversion to blood sugar. This results in a lower and more stable insulin level in the blood. The non-soluble fiber in vegetables increases the volume of the food and the feeling of satiety. This combination of soluble and non-soluble fiber gives you blood sugar control and reduces the feeling of hunger.

There is, however, a lot more to vegetables than fiber. They are also packed with antioxidants and phytochemicals that protect against various diseases. For example, dark green vegetables and brightly colored vegetables such as broccoli, cabbage, Brussels sprouts, bell peppers, and tomatoes protect against cancer, while the onion group (garlic, onion, scallion, leek, chives) offers similar protection and can help lower cholesterol and blood pressure.

Your best insurance against disease is a refrigerator filled with fresh vegetables, but don't forget frozen ones also have their place. They are a valuable source of nutrients and in fact often retain more vitamins than their fresh counterparts. Some canned vegetables are also useful: No kitchen should be without canned tomatoes, while more unusual canned vegetables such as artichoke hearts are convenient and taste great cooked with a little olive oil and lemon juice.

Take care when cooking vegetables. Boiling is not the best way to prepare them because so many water-soluble vitamins and trace minerals are discarded along with the water. Steaming is a much better method. You should also eat salads and raw vegetables as often as possible.

Legumes

Beans, lentils, and chickpeas are a valuable addition to any diet: They are certainly not just for vegetarians. Once you have decided to reduce your intake of potatoes, rice, and pasta dramatically, legumes will become very important to you. They are low-glycemic and contain a lot of protein, fiber, vitamins, minerals, and healthy fatty acids. If you want more stable blood sugar and lower insulin production, the answer is simple: Get to know your beans and lentils!

They have been proven to lower the level of LDL cholesterol and triglycerides in the blood and to increase the "good" HDL cholesterol. They protect against cancer and are rich in calcium and iron. They are also the best source of soluble fiber in food; this type of fiber increases the feeling of satiety and gives good blood sugar control. Once called "poor people's meat," legumes also have the added advantage of being a great value.

There are numerous types of beans and lentils to choose from, both dried and canned. Beans that you have soaked and cooked yourself do have a lower GI than canned beans, but the difference is not significant; both types are perfectly acceptable. If you do soak your own beans, it is a good idea to cook a large portion, as they will keep for days in the refrigerator and also freeze well. Dried lentils do not need to be soaked before cooking.

Fruit

Most types of fruit have a low glycemic effect, partly because of their high fiber content and partly because the natural sweetness of fruit comes from fructose. Fructose, or fruit sugar, has a very low GI, 19—far lower than sucrose (table sugar), with a GI of 68. Cherries and grapefruit have a particularly low GI; plums, peaches, pears, apples, oranges, grapes, strawberries, and other berries also have a low GI. Bananas and some tropical fruits have somewhat higher glycemic effect, so don't eat these too regularly.

You should eat more vegetables than fruit, but fruit is nonetheless very important to a balanced diet. As well as fiber, fruit is an excellent source of vitamins, minerals, and other antioxidants. Oranges contain a lot of potassium, folic acid, and vitamin C. Strawberries, raspberries, and kiwi fruit are even richer sources of vitamin C, while figs are a source of calcium. Several phytochemicals in fruit can also help protect against cancer.

Most people like the taste of fruit, and fresh fruit can satisfy your craving for something sweet without giving you a lot of fat or starch at the same time. A combination of yogurt, fruit, and nuts is a healthy between-meals snack.

Medium- and high-glycemic carbohydrates

These are the foods that form the reward part of your once-a-day reward meal. By this, I mean that they should be eaten in moderation, when for many people, particularly those who are overweight, these foods are a central part of their diet.

Bread

Bread is a very important part of food culture. Too important, one could argue, because it is often eaten as part of every meal. How healthy is bread for you? Well, we really do not need grain products at all to live a healthy and long life, but whole

Fiber

Although dietary fiber (an indigestible form of carbohydrate) contributes little energy, it plays a very important role in human health. Almost all the fiber that we get from our diet comes from vegetables, fruit, legumes, grains, and nuts. There are two main types of fiber: soluble and insoluble. Soluble fiber ensures the proper digestion of nutrients and enables the bowels to absorb carbohydrates more slowly, thus blood sugar rises at a steadier level over a longer period of time. Soluble fiber also lowers cholesterol and is prebiotic, i.e. it supports good intestinal health. Soluble fiber is found in beans and lentils, oats, vegetables, and fruit. Non-soluble dietary fiber, which is found mainly in whole grains, increases the volume of food and aids bowel function. It is believed that the fiber in our diet can prevent some forms of cancer, such as colon cancer, but this might also be due to other substances in fruit and vegetables.

Most people in the Western world consume much less than 20 g (³⁄₄ ounce) of fiber per day. The official recommendation is 30 g (about 1 ounce) daily. An easy way to increase your intake of dietary fiber is to eat two fruits and at least three to four servings of vegetables a day. Eating lentils and beans instead of potatoes and bread, for example, will also increase the amount of fiber in your diet. When you increase the amount of fiber in your diet, you should also increase your water intake, to ensure regular bowel function.

grains do contain protein, fiber, vitamins, and minerals. In that respect they contribute in a positive way to our diet, as long as they do not dominate and replace other foods. However, that is exactly what is happening today. Grain products such as refined wheat flour, bread, pasta, cakes, cookies, and cereals make up a substantial part of what we eat every day. These products contain a lot of energy and carbohydrates. They also tend to be made from highly refined flour, with little in the way of fiber, protein, vitamins, and minerals.

Ideally, we should not eat bread or grains at all, but it would be naive to think that we could cease doing it. Besides, bread and other baked products taste good. Instead we should regard bread as something that should be eaten in restricted amounts—and chosen with care.

Bread and flour products vary significantly in their glycemic effect, depending on the flour they are made of. The finer the flour, the quicker blood sugar and insulin will rise after consumption. The GL of bread per 100 g (3½ ounces) varies between 30 and 50. Unfortunately, most of the bread that is sold is highly refined and contains more than 80 percent fine wheat flour, which gives you a lot of energy, but little nourishment.

When buying bread do not be fooled by products described as "brown" or "multi-grain" bread. They generally contain mostly fine wheat flour because it is the cheapest raw material there is. The color of a bread does not necessarily indicate that it is a whole-grain product—if you use sufficient color (malt), you could make fine bread that is almost black. And a bread that is "multi-grain" need not contain any "whole" grains at all. What matters is how coarse and heavy the bread is. Whole grains weigh more than fine flour, and this is how you can assess how coarse a loaf of bread is. The coarser the bread, the lower the GL.

The type of grain is also important. Rye and barley give a lower GL than wheat. However, if you

Sweet but dangerous

Is there room for sweet things in a healthy diet? Of course there is. However, the source of sweetness you choose is very important. Sugars are part of the cellular structure of many foods such as whole fruit and vegetables. It is not these, but the vast amount of so-called added sugars—those found in honey, table sugar (and other sugars such as demerara, cane sugar, muscovado), fruit juices, baked goods, confectionery, convenience foods, and so on—that are causing so many of today's health problems. If you wish to lose weight or gain control of your blood sugar levels, wherever possible you should avoid products that contain sucrose, or table sugar; glucose, glucose syrup or corn syrup (these concentrated syrups are widely used by the food industry); honey (which contains glucose, fructose, and sucrose); and maltose, the sugar that is found in beer. As a rule of thumb, no more than 10 percent of your daily energy intake should come from added sugars. With an intake of 2000 calories, that would mean a maximum of 50 g (1¾ ounces) of added sugar a day. The average daily intake of added sugars in the Western world is far greater than this.

As you may know, the sugar contained in fruit is fructose. Fructose reacts differently in the body from other kinds of sugar. It is absorbed more slowly in the small intestine and cannot be converted into energy immediately. Fructose has a very small effect on blood sugar, and a low GI of 19 (the GI of sucrose is 68). I recommend that, wherever possible, you should substitute fructose or no-cal sweeteners for other sugars, but also that you reduce your consumption of sugar in all forms (see p. 167 for more on fructose). Fructose and artificial sweeteners are not a necessary part of any diet, they are just a better alternative to sugar. Fruit is also not recommended in unlimited quantities; in particular limit your intake of medium-glycemic fruits, such as bananas. In general I recommend no more than two pieces of fruit a day.

prefer wheat breads look for a heavy loaf that is labelled "stone-ground whole-wheat." Alternatively, you may be able to find bread made from spelt. Spelt is an ancient type of wheat that has become increasingly popular in recent years. It has roughly the same GL as whole wheat, i.e. relatively high, but it contains a bit more protein, more fiber, and more vitamins and minerals. It also seems to be tolerated better by those with poor tolerance to regular wheat.

Nuts and seeds such as sunflower, pumpkin, and flax will also reduce the GL of bread and add more protein, healthy fat, and fiber. Sourdough bread has a slightly lower GL than other breads, because acidity reduces the glycemic effect of foods.

Coarse bread is more expensive than bread made from highly refined flour, but remember that you pay a lot for air when you buy baguettes. Keep in mind though that even the coarsest bread will range from medium to high GL—it is never low GL.

Pasta

Many people are surprised to learn that pasta has a lower GI than bread. That is because pasta is normally made from durum wheat (semolina), which has a lower GI than regular wheat. Durum wheat flour is coarser and contains somewhat more protein. Also, the less you cook the pasta, the lower its GL. Pasta cooked until it is "al dente," which gives you something to chew on, is better for the blood sugar than pasta that has been cooked for longer.

Rather than choosing white pasta, opt for one made from whole-wheat durum wheat, as it contains more fiber, vitamins, and minerals than the more refined variety. It was once only available in health food shops but most supermarkets now sell it in the form of either fusilli or spaghetti. And don't forget the protein-enriched pasta discussed on page 39—it's a very good choice.

Pasta can also be made by using a proportion of other types of grain, such as barley, flour from white

lentils, mung beans, and soybeans, which gives a much lower GL. On the other hand, gluten-free pasta is normally made from corn, millet, or buckwheat, which gives it a higher GL. Always bear in mind that serving size is vital—many people eat pasta in over-large portions.

Rice

There is a wide—and confusing—array of rice varieties, but which of them is best for your blood sugar? Rice can vary from medium to high GI, depending on type and how it is cooked. Short-grained, sticky Asian (jasmine and sushi) rice has a high GL and should be avoided. Long-grain basmati rice is a better choice. "Parboiled" long-grain American rice also has a lower GL, as it is steamed before being processed further, which makes the rice less sticky and gives it a lower GL. As a rule of thumb: The stickier the rice is after it has been cooked, the higher the GL. Brown rice does not have a significantly lower GL than parboiled white rice but it does contain more of the whole grain hull and is richer in fiber, vitamins, and minerals, so it is the healthiest choice. Wild rice, which is not a rice but a type of grass, is another good choice as it has a low GL, lots of fiber, and a pleasant nutty taste.

Other grains

Oats Old-fashioned rolled oats (the ones with the big flakes) have a lower GL than the pre-cooked variety, so these are the better choice. You can use oats to make porridge of course, but oatmeal can also replace some of the wheat flour in many recipes, such as muffins, bread, pancakes, cookies, pie pastry, and pizzas.

Barley Barley has a pleasantly nutty taste and a lower GL than many other grains. It is therefore an excellent alternative to rice and potatoes, as a side dish or in soups and stews. Try it in place of rice when making risotto. You can also use it when you bake, but bear in mind that barley contains very little gluten so if you want bread that leavens and is elastic, you need to add 10 g (½ ounce) gluten flour per 100 g (5½ ounces) barley flour.

Buckwheat Roasted buckwheat kernels (also called "kasha") have a medium GL and are a good alternative to rice in cereals and porridge.

Bulgur and couscous Bulgur is coarsely chopped durum wheat that has been partially pre-cooked and dried; couscous is simply a finer variety of bulgur. Both grains take just a few minutes to prepare and are a good choice of grain, having a relatively low GL.

Quinoa Called the "mother grain" by the Incas, quinoa is high in protein and has a relatively low GL. It has a slightly nutty flavor and is a good alternative to rice in savory dishes. It is widely available in health food shops and some of the larger supermarkets.

Breakfast cereals

Breakfast cereals are easy and convenient; many people eat them every day. This is not something I recommend but if you are one of those people it is important to find a cereal that is minimally processed and unsweetened. This can be tricky, as most cereals are high-glycemic and prepared from highly processed grains. Corn flakes, for example, have a very high GL. Did you know that a 1-cup serving of corn flakes gives you a similar increase in blood sugar and insulin to an equal amount of pure sugar?

Opt for cereals that are high in fiber—All-Bran is a good example—and have no added sugar. Don't assume that because something has a "healthy" reputation it will be suitable for a low-glycemic lifestyle—muesli is often sweetened and most brands contain dried fruit, which has a high GL. A much better alternative is unsweetened muesli made from grains and seeds and with a minimal amount of dried fruit (preferably none at all).

Whichever cereal you choose, if you add milk and berries, chopped nuts, ground flaxseeds, or soy pieces, or a spoonful of yogurt, this will lower its GL. And if you must sweeten your cereal, use a little fructose—not sugar.

Potatoes

Many people find it strange that potatoes have a high GI—after all, they are a vegetable aren't they? Yes they are but the human body lacks the enzymes to digest raw potato and so it must be cooked. Cooking potato alters its starch content, making it more easily digestible. Cooked potato causes a rapid rise in blood sugar and insulin levels. It is worth bearing in mind that potatoes, along with grains, are one of the most efficient foods for fattening domestic animals.

By all means, have potatoes once in a while if you are happy with your weight. But steer clear of french fries and chips. They have been fried at high temperatures in plant oils and can contain harmful by-products from heated oil.

Fats and oils

Fat—the right kind of course—is a vital part of the Mediterranean diet. In the Food, health, and weight section I looked at why good fats are so important in achieving good health; the following guidance will help you translate that information into good choices at the supermarket.

Choosing fats and oils

Monounsaturated fat This should be the type of fat you eat most of, as monounsaturated fat increases good (HDL) cholesterol levels and helps keep down bad (LDL) cholesterol. Almonds, avocados, Brazil nuts, cashew nuts, hazelnuts, macadamia nuts, olives, peanuts, pecans, and pistachios are very rich in monounsaturated fat; a few nuts, together with some fruit, makes a healthy and satisfying snack. The healthiest types of oils are extra-virgin olive oil, cold-pressed canola oil, and avocado oil, as these contain mainly mono-unsaturated fat.

Omega-3, polyunsaturated fat Most of us get too little omega-3 fatty acids and should increase our intake. Omega-3s have many benefits; in particular they have a protective effect against cardiovascular disease, and because they are an essential component of the brain, they are thought to lift depression and even improve intelligence. The best source is oily fish such as salmon, sardines, mackerel, herring, and tuna, as well as cod liver oil (as a supplement). Flaxseed is the richest source of omega-3 in the plant world, with as much as 58 percent health-friendly omega-3 fatty acids. It has a pleasantly nutty taste, and adding 1 to 2 teaspoons of cold-pressed flaxseed oil to food just before you eat it will boost your omega-3 intake.

Omega-6, polyunsaturated fat Though essential, omega-6 fatty acids are consumed in far greater quantities than necessary in the modern world. Corn, sunflower, safflower, and soybean oils, and the margarines derived from them, are all high in omega-6s and are widely used both in home cooking and by the food industry. To reduce your intake, switch from using sunflower, corn, soy, and other refined oils and margarines to cold-pressed or extra-virgin oils—mainly olive oil—and avoid eating fried foods too frequently.

Saturated fat Many people eat far more saturated fat than they need, in the form of saturated fats from full-fat dairy products (milk, butter, cream, and cheese), meat, cakes, cookies, and pastries. Saturated fat is non-essential and thus not desirable in large quantities as it displaces the healthier and essential unsaturated fat. Moderate amounts of saturated fat will not do you any harm; it is when saturated fats are eaten to excess, as part of a high-glycemic diet, that problems arise.

Trans fats These man-made fats, also known as hydrogenated (or partially hydrogenated) vegetable oils and fats, should be avoided wherever possible. Trans fatty acids are associated with a greatly increased risk of heart disease and many other inflammatory and degenerative diseases. They are found in many margarines, vegetable shortenings, and yellow fat spreads, and are widely used in the food industry to increase the shelf life of foods. The majority of ready-made foods contain significant amounts of trans fats, so always check the labels and avoid foods that list "partially hydrogenated" (vegetable) oil among the ingredients.

In the kitchen

I grew up in Greece, in a family that really knew how to appreciate good food. My grandmother in particular was a good cook, yet I cannot remember that she ever used a recipe or consulted a cookbook. Much of what I know about cooking is thanks to her. I was allowed to be an apprentice in her kitchen, which is why today I am able to cook and create new recipes without using cookbooks. Unlike my grandmother, however, I have a considerable collection of cookbooks from around the world. I refer to them often, both for information and inspiration.

My grandmother's cooking was excellent, but the menu was relatively simple and traditional; it made full use of Greece's wide range of home-grown ingredients, in particular vegetables, fruit, legumes, and nuts. If you want to cook healthy, interesting food it is important to find out as much as you can about the ingredients that are available to you and to learn how to use them. Sadly, despite the fact that we have so many cookbooks and magazines that feature delicious recipes, it seems that many people feel that preparing a home-cooked meal is too much trouble, and they end up eating frozen pizza or takeout for dinner. To cook "from scratch" often means heating up a pasta sauce.

We have discovered exciting food from other cultures, but find it difficult to prepare this food ourselves. We have so many demands on our time —work, household chores, hobbies, and keeping up with friends—that we are always busy. When you get home from work, you have perhaps not given much thought to what you and the rest of the family should eat. You open the refrigerator and take a look inside. You see many different ingredients, but nothing that is suitable for dinner. So it's pizza again…

Planning is important if you want to eat well. If you do not plan ahead, it is even more important that you are able to cook with the ingredients you have on hand. This becomes much easier if you have a well-stocked pantry and have familiarized yourself with a few cooking techniques and basic recipes. This section will help you make the most of your time in the kitchen.

Kitchen equipment

If you are serious about cooking healthily, it is important to make sure that you have the appropriate utensils. In addition to good-quality pots and pans, knives and so on, I recommend a food processor, a hand-held electric blender, and a core temperature/meat thermometer: These are particularly useful for preparing simple healthy food. An ice cream machine is admittedly not a necessity, but I recommend it if you want to make delicious ice cream that isn't full of additives and doesn't cost a fortune. Many of the items in the following list are kitchen essentials and will help you prepare the recipes in this book. Some are optional but recommended for serious home cooks.

chef's knife with 8-inch blade
paring knife with 2-inch blade
filleting knife
serrated knife
carving knife
carving fork
knife sharpener
saucepans (large, medium, and
    small)
large nonstick skillet, with lid
small nonstick skillet (can also
    be used as an omelet pan)
baking dish (enameled cast
    iron or glass is good)
roasting pans
ridged grill pan
vegetable steamer
chopping boards (one for raw
    meat and fish, one for
    vegetables)
wooden spoons
slotted spoon
tongs

kitchen scissors
poultry shears
vegetable peeler
metal skewers
ladle
balloon whisk
cheese grater
zest grater
lemon squeezer
garlic press
pitter (for olives)
apple corer
can opener
measuring cups
measuring spoons
mortar and pestle
pepper mill
salt mill
kitchen scale
kitchen timer
mixing bowls
rubber spatula
baking sheet

9-inch cake pan
loaf pan
ramekins
large colander
strainer
airtight containers (for
    storing food)
disposable rubber gloves (for
    chopping chile peppers)
pastry brush
nailbrush (for cleaning mussels)
tweezers (for removing fish bones)
food processor
electric hand-held or regular
    blender
electric hand-held or stand mixer
core temperature thermometer
ice cream machine

Stocking your pantry, refrigerator, and freezer

A well-stocked kitchen makes it easy to prepare meals with minimum fuss and last-minute shopping. You are also more likely to experiment with exciting new recipes if you have most of the ingredients on hand. I keep a list of items I have run out of, so I can stock up next time I go shopping.

Remember that some items have a limited shelf life, so turn out your kitchen cupboards every two or three months. Nuts—including peanut butter—and seeds quickly become rancid, while dried herbs and spices lose their individual aromas. The following are suggestions for your shopping list.

Kitchen cupboards

sodium-reduced salt

whole peppercorns, black and white

oils: extra-virgin olive, cold-pressed canola, cold-pressed avocado, cold-pressed walnut, sesame

clarified butter (ghee): it keeps for months and tolerates high temperatures without burning

vinegars: white wine, red wine, balsamic, raspberry, cider, rice

sauces: soy, Tabasco, Worcestershire, mayonnaise, sweet chile, Chinese oyster, Thai fish

spices: allspice, anise seeds, caraway seeds, cardamom pods, cayenne pepper, chili powder, whole and ground cinnamon, cloves, ground coriander, ground cumin, curry powder, fennel seeds, powdered ginger, whole and ground nutmeg, turmeric, saffron

dried herbs: bay leaves, oregano, thyme, rosemary, marjoram, sage, tarragon, mint

vanilla beans and vanilla extract

reduced-sodium stock, ready-made concentrated stock, or vegetable bouillon powder

canned coconut milk

canned tomatoes

canned artichoke hearts

canned beans, chickpeas, lentils

dried lentils: red, brown, green

canned fish: anchovies, mackerel, sardines, tuna

nuts: whole and ground almonds, Brazil nuts, peanuts, pine nuts, pistachios, cashews, walnuts, pecans, macadamia nuts

natural peanut butter

seeds: sunflower, flax, pumpkin, sesame

dried apricots

chocolate: bittersweet (at least 70% cacao), unsweetened

onions

garlic

couscous

bulgur wheat

quinoa

steel-cut oats

various whole-grain flakes (rye, spelt, oatmeal)

roasted buckwheat kernels (kasha)

pearl barley

pasta: whole wheat spaghetti or fusilli, or protein-enriched pasta

rice: brown basmati, American long-grain parboiled rice, wild

flour: stone-ground whole-wheat, spelt, barley, soy, chickpea, rye, durum wheat (fine semolina)

thickeners: cornstarch, arrowroot

baking powder

dried yeast

fructose powder (fruit sugar)

white and red wine, port, sherry

Fruit bowl

lemons, limes

apples

berries (raspberries, blueberries, strawberries etc.)

pears

oranges, tangerines

peaches, nectarines

apricots

cherries

melon, watermelon

plums

grapefruit

kiwi fruit

grapes

pomegranates

passion fruit

Refrigerator

eggs

cold-pressed flaxseed oil

skim milk or soy milk

heavy cream, half-and-half,
    soy cream with 18% and 36%
    fat

crème fraîche, sour cream
    (reduced-fat if available)

yogurt: low-fat plain,
    fat-free fruit yogurt sweetened
    with fructose, or soy yogurt

cheese: cottage cheese, ricotta,
    fromage blanc, quark, feta,
    Parmesan, mature Cheddar,
    Gruyère

mustard: whole grain, Dijon

tomato paste

pesto

hummus and tahini (sesame seed
    paste)

curry paste

olives and olive paste

anchovy paste

horseradish

ginger

red and green chile peppers

fresh herbs: basil, cilantro, mint,
    thyme, parsley

vegetables such as eggplant,
    carrots, celery, zucchini,
    cucumber, red and green bell
    peppers, tomatoes, fennel,
    cabbage, broccoli, Brussels
    sprouts, cauliflower, salad
    greens (e.g. lettuce, chicory,
    arugula, watercress), leeks,
    scallions, mushrooms, spinach,
    asparagus, bean sprouts, green
    beans, onions, bok choy,
    radishes

In the freezer

If your freezer contains meat, fish,
    and vegetables, you will always
    have the basis for a good
    healthy meal in the house.

spinach

peas

broad (fava) beans

broccoli florets

berries: blackberries, blueberries,
    raspberries, strawberries,
    cranberries

shellfish: shrimp, squid (not
    breaded or battered)

fish: fillets of salmon, cod,
    haddock, turbot

chicken breasts and legs (skinless
    and boneless)

whole chicken

turkey breasts

ground turkey or chicken

duck breasts

meat: beef fillet, stewing beef,
    lean ground beef

lamb: leg of lamb, fillet, lean
    ground lamb

pork: fillet/tenderloin

homemade or other coarse
    whole-grain bread, sliced

Spice it up

You can make food more interesting by adding one or two fresh or dried herbs, spices, or other flavor enhancers. Below I've suggested some classic pairings, and some more unusual combinations that work surprisingly well. If you want to give something a Chinese flavor, use ginger and spring onions and finish with a few drops of soy sauce and sesame oil. For a Southeast Asian touch, include garlic and chiles, plus lime juice and Asian fish sauce. As well as making food taste great, herbs and spices contain a myriad of important bioactive ingredients. So don't let your herbs and spices gather dust in the cupboard—use them every day.

With fish Fennel, dill, parsley, tarragon, chives, cilantro, thyme, oregano, turmeric, mustard, curry, vinegar, lemon, lime, white wine

With shellfish Basil, parsley, dill, marjoram, chives, curry, cilantro, tarragon, oregano, thyme, chili, garlic, lemon, lime, mustard, coconut milk, white wine, sherry

With poultry Basil, oregano, garlic, chives, curry, tarragon, bay leaves, ginger, cinnamon, marjoram, thyme, chili, turmeric, vinegar, lemon, lime, orange, mustard, coconut milk, red wine, white wine, sherry

With beef Garlic, cumin, allspice, oregano, thyme, marjoram, curry, basil, cayenne, chili, bay leaves, mustard, horseradish, red wine, port

With lamb Garlic, oregano, basil, dill, rosemary, thyme, mint, allspice, cumin, red wine

With pork Garlic, dill, coriander, cumin, rosemary, thyme, cayenne, allspice, sage, ginger, lemon, curry, mustard, sherry, red and white wine

With game Garlic, juniper berries, thyme, oregano, bay leaves, allspice, rosemary, red wine, port

With eggs Tarragon, chives, cayenne, basil, curry

With dried beans and lentils Garlic, parsley, chives, coriander, cumin, curry, tarragon, marjoram, rosemary, thyme, sage, chili, cayenne, lemon

With asparagus Basil, dill, tarragon, chives, nutmeg

With peas Mint, basil, tarragon, chives, oregano, dill, marjoram, thyme

With broccoli, cauliflower, Brussels sprouts, cabbage Garlic, cumin, basil, tarragon, curry, marjoram, ginger, oregano, thyme

With spinach Garlic, nutmeg, dill, chives, basil, tarragon, coconut milk, chili

With eggplant Garlic, parsley, chili, oregano, marjoram, basil, mint, sage, thyme

With zucchini Garlic, parsley, oregano, dill, chives, tarragon, marjoram, basil, mint, sage, thyme

With green beans Parsley, basil, garlic, tarragon, dill, marjoram, rosemary

With mushrooms Garlic, parsley, oregano, marjoram, basil, chives, dill, tarragon

With bell peppers Garlic, cilantro, chives, oregano, thyme, marjoram

With tomatoes Garlic, chives, coriander, tarragon, oregano, marjoram, thyme, sage, chili, cayenne, mustard, cumin

Planning to eat well

You should always plan your meals in advance. You plan the agenda for a meeting or nothing would get done; you plan to have clean clothes to put on in the morning; why should food be an exception? Planning ahead saves time and money, and makes it easier to eat healthily. If you wait until you're hungry before you buy food, you're likely to end up with an expensive ready-made meal or takeout, packed with unhealthy fats and lacking in vitamins and minerals.

Making a weekly plan means that you can do most of your food shopping on one day, rather than trailing around the shops after work when you're tired and hungry. Also, by planning what you are going to eat in this way, you will waste far less food. A staggering amount of food is thrown away because it has languished in the refrigerator for too long. However, planning doesn't mean you can't be flexible: for example, if you see some lovely fresh fava beans at the market, you can easily swap them for the vegetables on your plan.

I've suggested a couple of weekly menu plans on pages 26–29; you can use these as inspiration for your own plans, but just remember that you must always include a variety of foods so you get a good range of essential vitamins and minerals.

Putting together a list of meals for the coming week also means you can do a lot of advance preparation. Why not prepare tomorrow's meals after you have had your dinner and relaxed for a while? That way, you avoid having to cook when you come home tired and hungry. If nearly everything is ready in advance, all you will need to do is to heat up the food.

Preparing larger amounts of food and having them later in the week is also a good idea. Why not set aside two or three hours on the weekend to cook casseroles, baked dishes, beans, and lentils? Or double the quantities of a recipe, then divide it into portions, and store in the refrigerator or freezer. That way, you will not have to prepare meals from scratch every night of the week.

Make ahead

Many of the recipes in this book can be prepared ahead of time or in larger quantities. These recipes are marked with this symbol and give advice on storage times. I've also included lots of tips on variations, so you won't feel as though you're eating the same meal two days in a row.

Preparing larger amounts of food makes good sense. Have you ever thought how professional chefs manage to cook so many different dishes in one day? By preparing a variety of broths, stocks, sauces, and garnishes and by doing as much advance preparation as possible, it becomes comparatively simple to put ingredients together in different combinations. This can save you both time and money. For example:

▶ From a basic meat sauce you can easily prepare 4 or 5 different meals (serve it with spaghetti; with tomato and avocado in fajitas; or as as the basis for moussaka or lasagne).

▶ Lentil and bean dishes are particularly good when cooked in advance. Reheat them and add herbs, spices, sauces, or other ingredients, such as grilled bacon, halved cherry tomatoes, or cubes of cheese.

▶ As well as preparing whole dishes in advance, also think about the various parts of a meal that could be used for other purposes: for example, the Almond and Garlic Sauce on page 104 is delicious served with fish or as a dip, so it's a good idea to make extra. This principle can be applied to many other sauces.

Basic cooking techniques

Making stock

The basis of so much cooking is a good broth or stock, and it is quite simple to prepare. Butchers and fishmongers will often give you bones for free.

To make a meat or chicken stock, roast the bones in the oven, together with chopped carrot, onion, celery, and leeks, until the bones are well browned. Transfer everything to a large pot, cover with water, bring to a boil, and simmer (skimming the surface often) over low heat for 1 to 6 hours, depending on how strongly flavored you want the stock. When the stock is ready, strain it into a clean saucepan and boil it to concentrate the flavor further, if desired. You can also boil it down to a syrupy consistency, which will give you a concentrated stock that can be used as a basis for sauces and soups.

To make fish stock, combine the shells from 1 pound shrimp with 8 ounces firm-fleshed fish, 1 chopped celery stalk, 1 thickly sliced small onion, 1 bay leaf, a squeeze of lemon juice, and 6 whole peppercorns in a pot and cover with 4 cups of cold water. Bring to a boil, then reduce the heat to low, cover, and simmer gently for 20 minutes, or until the fish falls apart. Strain carefully to remove any bones.

You will find a recipe for vegetable stock in the recipe for Greek Vegetable Soup on page 59. Alternatively, use organic bouillon powder.

Store stock in the refrigerator for 2 to 3 days (2 days for fish stock) or freeze it for up to 1 month. Concentrated stock can be frozen in ice cube trays.

Slow-roasting

Flavors develop in a fantastic way at low temperatures, and slow-roasted food is so tender and succulent that you will not need extra salt or rich sauces. However, cooking at low temperatures takes longer than at high temperatures, and this has to be taken into consideration before you begin.

Preheat the oven to its lowest setting—usually about 250°F. Put a roasting pan over low heat, add a few of tablespoons of olive oil plus herbs, garlic, or other flavorings, and then place the meat, poultry, or fish in the pan and insert an ovenproof meat thermometer into the thickest part. Remove from the oven when the core temperature has been reached: 130–150°F is fine for most meats that should be pink inside, whereas chicken and turkey should be 150–160°F.

The fricassée principle

This means that you cook meat, poultry, or fish together with vegetables in broth until everything is tender. To complete the dish, strain the broth, thicken it, and add your chosen seasonings, herbs, and spices. You can thicken the stock with cornstarch dissolved in a little cold water, or with egg yolks. If you use egg yolks, mix them with a few spoonfuls of the hot broth, then add them to the pot, and stir well. Do not let the mixture boil, or the egg yolks will curdle. You can also use a mixture of egg yolk, cream, or soy cream and thickener.

Alternatively, for a healthy thickener, add well-mashed or puréed red or yellow lentils or high-fiber vegetables, such as celery, tomatoes and/or onion. Serve the fricassée with mashed or puréed peas, beans, or lentils.

Ragouts and casseroles

There is not much difference between a ragout and a fricassée. The main difference is that when you make a ragout, you brown the ingredients first and often add tomatoes in one form or another (chopped tomatoes or tomato paste). Apart from that you follow the procedure for fricassée, but you do not need to strain the stock. Wine and more powerful spices and herbs such as chile peppers, mustard, allspice, and caraway seeds are often used in ragouts. Tougher cuts of meat such as shank and neck benefit from the long, slow cooking process, but the result is also good—and cooking times shorter—with poultry, better pieces of meat, vegetables, and fish.

Stir-frying

This cooking method originated in the Far East, but has now become very popular worldwide. It is a very good way of preparing healthy food, because it is quick and uses only a small amount of oil. The best oils for stir-frying are extra-virgin olive oil or sesame oil, which are rich in monounsaturated fat and tolerate quick heating better than oils with a high proportion of polyunsaturated fat, such as sunflower oil, soy oil, or corn oil. As the cooking time is so quick, you should always choose tender cuts of meat (preferably fillet), fish, or poultry.

Frying is bad news

Frying and deep frying are two of the most popular cooking methods. Unfortunately, they are also the most harmful cooking methods. The health hazard is a result of quick oxidation and other chemical changes that take place when oils are exposed to high temperatures, light and air. The chemicals these reactions produce are downright toxic. If you only use oil for frying very occasionally, your body can handle the toxins. Used every week—or even every day, as many people do—these waste substances accumulate in our cells and can trigger illnesses such as heart disease or cancer.

Should we then just stop frying and deep frying completely? Ideally, yes, though few of us are likely to do this. Therefore it is useful to know which fats are the least harmful for frying and deep frying. Polyunsaturated fat does not tolerate high temperatures well. Fish fat and the fat in most vegetable oils is polyunsaturated and is not suitable for frying. Consequently, you should avoid frying fatty fish. Monounsaturated and saturated fats tolerate high temperatures better. Olive oil and sesame oil mainly contain monounsaturated fat, and tolerate frying at low temperatures relatively well, but not deep frying. If you must fry at high temperatures or deep-fry, clarified butter (ghee) and unrefined coconut oil are preferable (although they contain a lot of saturated fat, they are stable at high temperatures and produce fewer harmful substances).

Avoid frying with lard, which consists almost wholly of saturated fat. Also avoid using cheaper margarines and hydrogenated oils. These are often totally artificial products, and are likely to contain trans fatty acids.

If you wish to fry food, stir-frying is your best option, because the fat and the food are only exposed to high temperatures for a short time. Another alternative is to cook your ingredients in a little stock or boiling water, and then fry them for a very short time at a low temperature.

First you need to chop or slice all your ingredients and have them ready by a large, deep skillet or wok. Heat the pan to a high temperature, add a little oil, then add your main ingredient, and stir over the heat until it begins to color (chicken and other poultry should be cooked through); remove from the pan. Now add the vegetables, stirring all the time. You should fry tough vegetables such as broccoli, cauliflower, onion, and bell peppers first, and then add more tender vegetables, such as scallions, asparagus, and snow peas. Put the main ingredient back in the pan and season to taste. Soy sauce, ginger, chiles, sesame oil, and garlic are commonly used ingredients, but you can also give the food a Mediterranean touch by using garlic, pesto, oregano, thyme, and tarragon or an Indonesian touch by adding peanut butter and coconut milk.

Meatballs and fishcakes

Lean meat, game, poultry, fish, and shellfish, ground or very finely chopped, make a good, simple supper dish. Quality and freshness are very important, so don't just focus on price. If you buy pre-ground meat, make sure it's not full of fat or ice/water. Add herbs or spices, finely chopped onion, garlic, or any other vegetables and one or two eggs. Mix everything well. If you want to "stretch" the mixture, don't add bread crumbs or flour: Use rolled oats or mashed red lentils instead. Allow the mixture to rest for about 20 minutes, or for several hours, in the refrigerator. Shape the mixture into balls or patties and cook them over low heat in a nonstick skillet until they are cooked through. At a low temperature, flavors will develop better and the need for salt and fat will be reduced.

Simple desserts

Choose low-glycemic, fiber-rich fruit such as apples, pears, citrus fruits, raspberries, blackberries, strawberries, grapes, cherries, kiwi fruit, plums, peaches, nectarines, or melons. Try:

- ▶ Mixed strawberries, raspberries, and blueberries
- ▶ Green grapes, sliced kiwi fruit, and melon balls
- ▶ Orange slices sprinkled with cinnamon
- ▶ Strawberries sprinkled with a little black pepper or balsamic vinegar
- ▶ Mashing, puréeing, or stewing fruit (with spices and fructose if you like) to make fruit soup
- ▶ Puréeing fruit to make a sauce to go with ricotta, yogurt, or ice cream
- ▶ Plain yogurt with fruit; it's filling and healthy
- ▶ Unsweetened yogurt flavored with vanilla extract and fructose. Swirl in some crushed berries or sprinkle with chopped walnuts or pistachios and drizzle with honey.

The recipes

Before you begin cooking any of the recipes please note the following:

▶ When a recipe includes salt, I recommend that you use low-sodium or reduced-sodium salt. Most of us consume far more salt than we need: We require only about 1 g of salt a day, yet the average intake is far higher. If you gradually reduce the amount of salt you add to your food you will begin to taste far more of the natural flavors of the ingredients and will soon get into the habit of using less.

▶ Unless a recipe states otherwise, "pepper" means freshly ground black pepper from the mill.

▶ Where a recipe includes olive oil, this refers to extra-virgin olive oil. "Extra-virgin" means that the oil is cold pressed in a natural way and has not been processed at high temperatures.

▶ If you do not use your own homemade stock or broth for recipes, use low-sodium broth, which is available in supermarkets. Alternatively, use vegetable bouillon powder, which is available in health food shops and some supermarkets.

▶ Many of the recipes that are oven-cooked are heated at a low temperature. This produces lovely succulent meat, poultry or fish (see page 53). However, it is best to use a core temperature/meat thermometer to ensure the meat is cooked all the way through. If you do not have a thermometer, pierce the thickest part of the meat with a thin metal skewer and if the juices run clear it is cooked.

▶ Where a recipe includes a "make ahead" symbol this indicates that the dish can be refrigerated or frozen. Unless the instructions state otherwise, all dishes should be cooled and then placed in an airtight container prior to chilling or freezing. Frozen food should be thoroughly defrosted before being reheated.

▶ At the end of each recipe you will find the nutritional information. The Glycemic Load (GL) per serving has been calculated based on the total carbohydrate amount in grams, multiplied by the Glycemic Index (GI) of the main blood-sugar-influencing ingredient(s) and divided by 100. If the carbohydrate source is solely very low-glycemic vegetables, the GL is practically zero. Since many of the recipes in this book include significant amounts of protein and/or fat, and also lemon juice or yogurt—all known to reduce the GI and thus the GL—they have a very low GL of less than 6.5 per serving. There are of course a number of recipes that include higher GL carbs; these are designed to be part of your reward meal of the day.

◄ Cucumber Soup with Shrimp

SERVES 4

2 cucumbers

1²⁄₃ cups chicken broth

²⁄₃ cup reduced-fat crème fraîche
or sour cream

Juice of ½ lemon

Salt and pepper

½ small red chile pepper,
finely chopped

½ inch piece fresh ginger, finely
chopped

3 tablespoons sweet chile sauce

2 sprigs dill, finely chopped

8 ounces cooked shelled shrimp

A refreshing summer first course, this soup features hot and spicy shrimp as a source of protein.

1 Peel the cucumbers and chop coarsely. Using a food processor or blender, purée the cucumbers, broth, crème fraîche, and lemon juice until completely smooth. Season to taste with salt and pepper, then cover, and chill for at least 2 hours.

2 Mix the chile, ginger, chile sauce, and dill and season to taste. Add the shrimp and marinate in the refrigerator for 1 hour.

3 Serve the soup, topped with the shrimp, in chilled bowls.

PER SERVING GLYCEMIC LOAD 0; PROTEIN 14 G; CARBOHYDRATES 8 G; FAT 6 G (INCLUDES 3 G SATURATED FAT); FIBER 1 G

Greek Fish Soup

SERVES 6

6 tablespoons olive oil

1 onion, chopped

1 cup chopped leeks, white
parts only

½ fennel bulb, chopped

3 parsley stalks

1 bay leaf

2 sprigs fresh thyme or
1 teaspoon dried

Scant 2 cups dry white wine

Salt and pepper

1 pound mussels in
their shells

1 pound shrimp in
their shells

3½ pounds fish fillets
(preferably 3 or 4 different types)

This Greek version of bouillabaisse is known as fisherman's soup or kakavia. It is traditionally made from a mixture of different types of fish and shellfish—the catch of the day!

1 Heat the oil in a large saucepan over low heat. Add the onion and cook until soft but not brown, 5 to 10 minutes. Add the leeks, fennel, herbs, wine, and 3 cups water and bring to a boil. Add a pinch of salt, reduce the heat, and simmer for 45 minutes.

2 Meanwhile, clean the mussels thoroughly, discarding any that are open or have broken shells. Rinse and shell the shrimp. Cut the fish into 1½- to 2-inch pieces and sprinkle lightly with salt. Set aside.

3 Strain the vegetable liquid through a sieve into a clean saucepan, pressing down on the vegetables to extract as much liquid as possible. Bring the vegetable broth back to a boil, then reduce the heat, add the fish, and simmer for 5 to 10 minutes. Add the mussels and simmer until all the shells are open, about 5 minutes. Add the shrimp and simmer until they are opaque, a minute or two. Season to taste with salt and pepper and serve at once.

PER SERVING GLYCEMIC LOAD 0; PROTEIN 69 G; CARBOHYDRATES 9 G; FAT 19 G (INCLUDES 3 G SATURATED FAT); FIBER 1 G

Greek Vegetable Soup

SERVES 4

¼ cup olive oil

2 onions, finely chopped

2 garlic cloves, crushed

3 cups shredded green cabbage

3 carrots, diced

3 celery stalks, chopped

1 15-ounce can chickpeas, rinsed

6 cups vegetable broth or water

1 15-ounce can chopped tomatoes

¼ cup chopped fresh parsley

Salt and pepper

¼ cup crumbled feta cheese

This is a substantial and satisfying soup, with protein from the chickpeas and feta cheese.

1 Put the olive oil in a large saucepan over low heat, add the onions and garlic, cover and cook until the onions are soft but not brown, 10 minutes. Add the cabbage and continue to cook for another 5 minutes.

2 Add the carrots, celery, and chickpeas, stir well, and cook until the vegetables begin to soften, about 5 minutes.

3 Add the broth or water and stir well. Increase the heat, and bring the soup to a boil. Cover the saucepan, lower the heat, and leave the soup to simmer for 30 minutes. Add the tomatoes and a little salt and pepper and simmer for another 20 minutes.

4 Stir in the parsley, and then ladle the soup into bowls or soup plates. Sprinkle the feta cheese over the soup and serve hot.

PER SERVING GLYCEMIC LOAD 7; PROTEIN 12 G; CARBOHYDRATES 55 G; FAT 18 G (INCLUDES 3 G SATURATED FAT); FIBER 12 G

 MAKE AHEAD Prepare up to step 3 and store in the refrigerator for up to 3 days. This soup can also be frozen.

Broccoli and Cauliflower Soup

SERVES 6

3 tablespoons olive oil

½ onion, sliced

1 head broccoli,
separated into florets

1 head cauliflower,
separated into florets

4 cups vegetable broth or water

Salt and pepper

½ cup half-and-half or
plain yogurt

This comforting, pale green soup is packed with vitamins and minerals, quick to make, and very versatile. Chopped fresh herbs are a tasty addition to the basic recipe. Just before serving you could also add a few drops of extra-virgin olive oil or cold-pressed flaxseed, pumpkin, or avocado oil—do not boil the soup after you have added the oil. To make a light meal, add some protein: shredded cooked chicken, strips of ham, chopped boiled egg, or a poached egg.

1 Heat the olive oil in a large saucepan over low heat, add the onion and cook until soft, 5 to 10 minutes. Add the broccoli and cauliflower and cook for a few minutes to soften. Add the broth or water and simmer until the vegetables are just tender, 8 to 10 minutes.

2 Blend in a food processor or blender until smooth. Season to taste with salt and pepper. Stir in the cream or yogurt, or pour the soup into bowls and swirl in the cream.

PER SERVING GLYCEMIC LOAD 0; PROTEIN 6 G; CARBOHYDRATES 20 G; FAT 10 G (INCLUDES 2 G SATURATED FAT); FIBER 6 G

 MAKE AHEAD This can be made a day in advance—but do not add the cream until serving. Store in the refrigerator.

Rich Tomato Soup

SERVES 4

1 tablespoon clarified butter

1 small onion, finely chopped

About 1 pound tomatoes, chopped

2 15-ounce cans chopped tomatoes

2 cups vegetable broth

½ small red chile pepper, seeded and chopped

1 tablespoon chopped fresh thyme leaves

2 tablespoons chopped fresh parsley, plus extra for garnish

1 garlic clove, finely chopped

1 ripe avocado, peeled and diced

2 tablespoons grated Parmesan cheese (optional)

Salt and pepper

Pinch of fructose powder

1 tablespoon olive oil

Tomatoes are packed with lycopene, a micronutrient with potent anti-cancer properties. To serve this as a light meal, add a source of protein, such as cubed turkey or chicken, cooked shrimp, steamed fish fillets or 1 or 2 halved boiled eggs per person.

1 Heat the butter in a large saucepan, add the onion, and cook until soft, 5 to 10 minutes. Add the fresh tomatoes, stir well, then add the canned tomatoes and broth, and simmer for about 15 minutes.

2 Reduce the heat to very low and blend with a hand-held blender or in a food processor. Add the chile, herbs, garlic, avocado (reserving a little for the garnish), and Parmesan, if using, and blend again. Add salt, pepper, and fructose to taste. Serve in warmed bowls, with the olive oil and a little parsley and avocado spooned on top.

PER SERVING GLYCEMIC LOAD 0; PROTEIN 5 G; CARBOHYDRATES 27 G; FAT 14 G (INCLUDES 3 G SATURATED FAT); FIBER 8 G

MAKE AHEAD Make the basis of the soup (step 1) a day ahead. Reheat until piping hot, and then stir in the chile and other flavorings. This soup can be frozen, but this should be done after step 1.

Mushroom Soup with Goat Cheese

SERVES 4

About 1 pound mushrooms

1 tablespoon clarified butter

1 small onion or
2 shallots, chopped

1 garlic clove, finely chopped

1 tablespoon fresh thyme leaves
or ½ teaspoon dried

3⅓ cups vegetable or chicken
broth

Scant 1 cup half-and-half

3½ ounces semisoft goat cheese,
rind removed

1 ripe avocado

Salt and pepper

7 ounces smoked ham,
cut into thin strips

Fresh herbs or herb oil
(page 68), for garnish

Rich, autumnal mushroom soup becomes a complete meal with the addition of goat cheese. Vegetarians could omit the ham and use extra cheese. Use any type of mushrooms for this soup, such as half cultivated mushrooms and half wild. You can also add a handful of dried mushrooms to boost the flavor: Soak them in hot water for 30 minutes before starting the recipe.

1 Clean the mushrooms; if they are very dirty you may need to rinse them. Chop or slice them.

2 Melt half of the butter in a large saucepan and add half of the mushrooms, the onion, and the garlic. Cook over medium heat until golden brown, about 10 minutes, then add the thyme, and cook for a few more minutes. Add the broth and half-and-half and simmer for 5 minutes.

3 Crumble the cheese into the soup and leave to melt over low heat.

4 Peel and chop the avocado and add to the soup. Blend until completely smooth, using a hand-held blender or food processor. Season to taste with salt and pepper.

5 Melt the remaining ½ tablespoon butter in a skillet over medium heat. Add the remaining mushrooms and cook until golden brown, about 10 minutes. Pour the hot soup into 4 warmed bowls. Put some of the mushrooms and ham into each bowl and sprinkle with fresh herbs.

PER SERVING GLYCEMIC LOAD 0; PROTEIN 19 G; CARBOHYDRATES 20 G; FAT 25 G (INCLUDES 12 G SATURATED FAT); FIBER 5 G

 MAKE AHEAD Prepare up to end of step 2, and then store in the refrigerator for up to 2 days or freeze.

Gazpacho

SERVES 4

About 2 cups tomato juice

Scant 1 cup vegetable broth

2 shallots, finely chopped

1 cucumber, peeled and grated

1 small green bell pepper, finely chopped

1 small red bell pepper, finely chopped

½ green chile pepper, seeded and finely chopped

2 tablespoons chopped fresh parsley

1 garlic clove, chopped

1 teaspoon Worcestershire sauce

1 teaspoon fructose powder

1 tablespoon olive oil

1 teaspoon cold-pressed flaxseed oil

1 to 2 drops Tabasco sauce

½ teaspoon salt

Black pepper

1 ripe tomato, finely diced

1 tablespoon finely chopped fresh chives

¼ cup crumbled feta cheese

Here is my version of the Spanish classic. Some people serve the garnishes in small bowls; optional garnishes include chopped scallions or chives, chopped hard-boiled eggs, and finely diced cucumber.

1 Put 1 cup of the tomato juice in a food processor with the broth, shallots, cucumber, bell peppers, chile, parsley, garlic, Worcestershire sauce, fructose, and olive oil. Blend until smooth. Add up to 1 cup additional tomato juice to get the consistency you want. Place in the refrigerator for at least 2 hours.

2 To serve, stir in the flaxseed oil, Tabasco, salt, and pepper to taste. Pour into chilled bowls and add a few ice cubes if you wish. Garnish with the diced tomato, chives, and feta cheese.

PER SERVING GLYCEMIC LOAD 2; PROTEIN 4 G; CARBOHYDRATES 14 G; FAT 7 G (INCLUDES 2 G SATURATED FAT); FIBER 2 G

MAKE AHEAD Prepare through step 1 and store the soup for up to 2 days in the refrigerator.

Provençal Chicken and Vegetable Soup

SERVES 4

SOUP

1 leek

2 carrots

1 celery stalk

1 zucchini

10 green beans

4 large ripe tomatoes

2 tablespoons clarified butter

2 sprigs fresh thyme or
½ teaspoon dried

1 bay leaf

4 cups chicken broth

4 boneless, skinless chicken breast
halves (about 5 ounces each),
cut into thin strips

Salt and pepper

PISTOU

Large bunch basil

2 garlic cloves

2 tablespoons freshly
grated Parmesan cheese

Scant ½ cup olive oil

Salt and pepper

Inspired by a classic vegetable soup from the south of France, this is a light version that includes chicken for a good balance of protein and carbohydrates—and it's ready in 15 minutes! A swirl of basil and garlic pistou is an aromatic finishing touch; use ready-made pesto if you like.

1 To make the soup, cut the leek (white and light green parts), carrots, celery, zucchini, green beans, and tomatoes into ½-inch pieces. Heat the butter in a large saucepan over low heat and add all of the vegetables except the tomatoes. Add 3 tablespoons water and cover with a lid. Cook gently until the water has evaporated, about 5 minutes, and then add the thyme, bay leaf, and broth. Bring to a boil, and then simmer until the vegetables are tender, about 5 minutes.

2 Meanwhile, make the pistou. Put the basil, garlic, and Parmesan into a food processor and blend briefly. With the machine running, gradually add the olive oil, blending until smooth. Season to taste with salt and pepper.

3 Add the chicken to the soup and simmer until the chicken is cooked through, 3 to 4 minutes. Stir in as much of the pistou as you want, then add the tomatoes, and season to taste with salt and pepper.

PER SERVING GLYCEMIC LOAD 2; PROTEIN 38 G; CARBOHYDRATES 16 G; FAT 33 G (INCLUDES 8 G SATURATED FAT); FIBER 5 G

MAKE AHEAD Make double quantities of soup (step 1) and freeze for up to 1 month. Reheat until piping hot, then add the chicken, and cook through; add tomatoes just before serving. The pistou can be made up to 4 days ahead and stored in the refrigerator.

Chickpea Soup with Herb Oil and Feta Cheese

SERVES 4

SOUP

1¾ cups dried chickpeas

3 tablespoons olive oil

1 large onion, chopped

1 tablespoon cornstarch

Juice of 1 lemon

3 tablespoons chopped fresh parsley

Salt and pepper

¼ cup crumbled feta cheese

HERB OIL

Scant ½ cup olive oil

1 large bunch fresh herbs (such as basil, thyme, cilantro), chopped

½ cup freshly grated Parmesan cheese

Serve a crisp green salad on the side to make this substantial soup into a complete meal. Instead of feta cheese, you could sprinkle finely grated Parmesan as a finishing touch.

1 Soak the chickpeas in a generous amount of water overnight.

2 Heat the olive oil in a large saucepan over low heat, add the onion, and cook until it begins to turn golden, 10 to 15 minutes. Rinse the chickpeas in a colander and add to the saucepan. Add enough water to cover the chickpeas by about 2 inches and bring to a boil. Reduce the heat and simmer, skimming occasionally, until the chickpeas are very tender, about 1½ hours.

3 Meanwhile, make the herb oil. Blend the olive oil, herbs, and Parmesan with a blender until they form a coarse, pesto-like paste.

4 Mix the cornstarch with the lemon juice and stir into the soup. Add the parsley and a little salt and pepper to taste. Transfer 2 ladlefuls of the soup to a deep bowl and blend briefly with a hand-held blender; the chickpeas should be crushed, not puréed. Stir this back into the soup.

5 Serve the soup in warmed bowls, sprinkled with a little feta cheese and 1 tablespoon of the herb oil.

PER SERVING GLYCEMIC LOAD 13; PROTEIN 18 G; CARBOHYDRATES 57 G; FAT 20 G (INCLUDES 4 G SATURATED FAT); FIBER 14 G

MAKE AHEAD This soup can be stored in the refrigerator for up to 3 days. It also freezes well for up to 3 months. The herb oil can be stored in the refrigerator for up to 3 days: It can be used when cooking fish (page 103) or poultry (page 114).

Greek Bean Soup

SERVES 6

1 cup cannellini beans
or other dried white beans

10 cups strong chicken or
vegetable broth

2 bay leaves

1 sweet onion, finely chopped

2 garlic cloves, crushed

2 carrots, diced

1 celery stalk, finely chopped
(reserve any leaves for garnish)

3 or 4 plum tomatoes, peeled,
seeded, and chopped, or 1 cup
canned chopped tomatoes

Juice of 1 lemon

6 tablespoons olive oil

Salt and pepper

1 teaspoon cold-pressed
flaxseed oil (optional)

¼ cup finely chopped
fresh parsley

In Greece, this is known as fassoláda, *and for most Greeks it's the closest thing to a national dish.*

1 Soak the beans in a generous amount of water overnight.

2 Drain the beans and put them in a large saucepan. Add the broth and the bay leaves. Bring to a boil, then reduce the heat, and simmer for 1½ hours.

3 Add the onion, garlic, carrots, and celery. Simmer for 30 minutes.

4 Add the tomatoes, lemon juice, and 3 tablespoons of the olive oil. Season with salt and pepper. Simmer until the beans are very soft, 30 minutes.

5 Remove from the heat, taste, and adjust the seasoning. Ladle into bowls and drizzle the remaining 3 tablespoons olive oil and the flaxseed oil over the top. Sprinkle with parsley and garnish with celery leaves if you wish. Serve hot.

PER SERVING GLYCEMIC LOAD 6; PROTEIN 11 G; CARBOHYDRATES 28 G; FAT 14 G
(INCLUDES 2 G SATURATED FAT); FIBER 7 G

MAKE AHEAD If anything, this improves if made a day ahead. Or make double quantities and freeze for up to 3 months.

Lentil Soup with Avocado and Turkey

SERVES 4

1½ cups dried green lentils

4 cups chicken or vegetable broth

4 tablespoons olive oil

1 onion, finely chopped

2 garlic cloves, finely chopped

2 tablespoons chopped fresh
thyme or 1 tablespoon dried

1 ripe avocado, peeled and
chopped

A little fresh lemon juice

Salt and pepper

1½ cups thinly sliced cooked
turkey breast

2 to 3 tablespoons torn fresh basil

Lentils are very nutritious—a good source of protein and fiber, as well as important minerals such as iron, zinc, and magnesium. The turkey adds extra protein to make a soup that is also a meal. Instead of the turkey, you could add 4 slices of grilled and crumbled lean bacon or ½ cup crumbled feta cheese. You could also include sun-dried tomatoes or Roasted Tomatoes (page 135).

1 Rinse the lentils thoroughly in a colander, then place in a large saucepan, add the broth, and bring to a boil. Reduce the heat and simmer until the lentils are soft, 25 to 35 minutes.

2 Meanwhile, put 2 tablespoons of the olive oil in a saucepan over low heat, add the onion and garlic, cover, and cook until the onion is translucent, 10 minutes. Add the thyme and stir until fragrant, a minute or two.

3 Add to the pan with the lentils, and then blend briefly with a hand-held blender; do not overblend. Add the avocado and blend again. If the soup is too thick, add a little broth or water. Season to taste with lemon juice, salt, and pepper.

4 Place the turkey breast in 4 warmed soup plates and pour the hot soup on top. Drizzle the remaining 2 tablespoons olive oil onto the soup, then add the basil, and serve at once.

PER SERVING GLYCEMIC LOAD 9; PROTEIN 33 G; CARBOHYDRATES 51 G; FAT 26 G (INCLUDES 4 G SATURATED FAT); FIBER 15 G

MAKE AHEAD This freezes well, so why not make a double quantity—but do not add the avocado and turkey until you are ready to serve. Alternatively, store in the refrigerator for up to 3 days.

Avocado Foam with Chicken

SERVES 4

2 tablespoons olive oil

4 boneless, skinless chicken breast halves (about 5 ounces each)

Salt and pepper

2 tablespoons chopped fresh herbs, such as basil, dill, cilantro, parsley, plus extra for garnish

1 tablespoon clarified butter

1 small onion or 2 shallots, chopped

½ teaspoon curry powder

1 tablespoon chopped fresh thyme or ½ teaspoon dried

½ small red chile pepper, seeded and finely chopped

3⅓ cups chicken broth

Scant 1 cup half-and-half

2 ripe avocados

½ teaspoon fructose powder

This gently spiced soup, with a generous helping of chicken, is a meal in itself. Cooking chicken at a low temperature gives a tender, juicy result.

1 Preheat the oven to 250°F or the lowest setting.

2 Heat the oil in a skillet, preferably nonstick, over high heat. Add the chicken breasts and cook until browned, 3 to 5 minutes per side. Season the chicken with a little salt and pepper and transfer to a roasting pan with the herbs. Roast in the oven for 25 to 30 minutes, or until the juices run clear when the chicken is pierced with a thin skewer.

3 Meanwhile, melt the butter in a saucepan over low heat, add the onion, and cook until translucent, 5 to 10 minutes. Add the curry powder, thyme, and chile and cook for 1 minute. Add the broth and half-and-half and simmer for 5 minutes.

4 Peel and chop the avocados and add to the soup, along with the fructose. Blend the soup until it is completely smooth and foamy. Season to taste with salt and pepper.

5 Slice the chicken into thin strips and place in 4 warmed soup plates. Pour the warm soup around the chicken and sprinkle with fresh herbs.

PER SERVING GLYCEMIC LOAD 0; PROTEIN 38 G; CARBOHYDRATES 15 G; FAT 33 G (INCLUDES 10 G SATURATED FAT); FIBER 7 G

Salade Niçoise with Grilled Seafood

DRESSING

3 tablespoons red wine vinegar

1 tablespoon Dijon mustard

1 tablespoon anchovy paste

½ teaspoon dried thyme

½ teaspoon fructose powder

5 tablespoons olive oil

SALAD

10 ounces tuna steak,
cut into 4 pieces

1 yellow zucchini,
cut into ¼-inch-thick slices

12 large scallops

8 large shelled shrimp, halved
lengthwise

7 ounces thin French
green beans, halved

1 tablespoon olive oil

1 red bell pepper,
seeded and cut into strips

1 head lollo rosso or romaine
lettuce, leaves separated

1½ cups yellow or red
cherry tomatoes, halved

⅔ cup pitted small green olives

This is an impressive and colorful main course salad. Instead of tuna, you could use fillets of red mullet.

1 To make the dressing, combine the vinegar, mustard, anchovy paste, thyme, fructose, and olive oil in a small bowl and emulsify with a hand-held blender. Alternatively, shake the ingredients together in a screwtop jar.

2 Place the tuna and zucchini on a baking sheet and brush on both sides with about 2 tablespoons of the dressing. Put the scallops and shrimp in a bowl and mix with 2 tablespoons of the dressing. Leave both to marinate for at least 15 minutes.

3 Bring a medium saucepan of lightly salted water to a boil. Drop the beans into the water and cook until tender but still bright green, about 3 minutes. Drain in a colander and rinse under cold water until cool. Transfer the beans to a bowl and add 2 tablespoons of the dressing. Set aside.

4 Heat the olive oil in a medium skillet and cook the red pepper over medium heat until soft, about 5 minutes. Set aside.

5 Preheat the grill to high. (If cooking indoors, heat a ridged grill pan or heavy skillet over high heat.) Grill the tuna, zucchini, shrimp, and scallops until the tuna is browned on the outside but still red in the center and the zucchini, shrimp, and scallops are just cooked through, about 2 minutes on each side.

6 Make a bed of lettuce leaves on 4 plates. Divide the scallops, shrimp, tuna, zucchini, beans, red pepper, tomatoes, and olives among the plates. Spoon a little dressing over each plate and serve the remaining dressing on the side.

PER SERVING GLYCEMIC LOAD 0; PROTEIN 32 G; CARBOHYDRATES 16 G; FAT 27 G (INCLUDES 4 G SATURATED FAT); FIBER 5 G

Smoked Salmon, Cauliflower, and Chickpea Salad

SERVES 4

SALAD

1 small head cauliflower (about 1 pound), separated into florets

1 15-ounce can chickpeas, rinsed and drained

6 ounces smoked salmon, cut into strips

2 hard-boiled eggs, sliced or chopped

DRESSING

5 tablespoons fromage blanc or quark

2 tablespoons olive oil

Small bunch fresh dill, chopped

Juice of 1 lemon

½ teaspoon fructose powder

Salt and pepper

A delicious protein-rich salad, this makes the perfect lunch or dinner when time is at a premium.

1 Bring a large saucepan of lightly salted water to a boil. Cook the cauliflower in the water until just tender, 3 to 5 minutes. Drain in a colander and set aside to cool.

2 To make the dressing, mix together the fromage blanc, oil, dill, lemon juice, and fructose and season with salt and pepper.

3 Combine the cauliflower and chickpeas in a salad bowl and add the smoked salmon and eggs. Pour the dressing on top and gently mix everything together. Serve at once.

PER SERVING GLYCEMIC LOAD 1; PROTEIN 22 G; CARBOHYDRATES 31 G; FAT 13 G (INCLUDES 2 G SATURATED FAT); FIBER 9 G

Tuna, Chickpea, and Avocado Salad

SERVES 4

DRESSING

4 tablespoons olive oil

2 tablespoons white wine vinegar

1 teaspoon Dijon mustard

½ teaspoon fructose powder

2 tablespoons freshly grated Parmesan cheese

Salt and pepper

SALAD

2 avocados

1 12-ounce can tuna in water, drained and flaked

1 15-ounce can chickpeas, rinsed and drained

1 red onion, cut into thin wedges

2 tablespoons finely chopped cornichons

1 tablespoon chopped fresh dill

This salad is simplicity itself, but for an even quicker tuna salad, mix the tuna with hard-boiled egg, finely chopped onion and cornichons, and a few tablespoons of fromage blanc.

1 To make the dressing, mix together the oil, vinegar, mustard, fructose, and Parmesan using a hand-held blender. Season with salt and pepper.

2 Halve the avocados and remove the pits. Scoop out the flesh and cut into dice.

3 Combine the avocado, tuna, chickpeas, red onion, cornichons, and dill in a salad bowl. Pour the dressing on top and gently mix everything together before serving.

PER SERVING GLYCEMIC LOAD 4; PROTEIN 31 G; CARBOHYDRATES 36 G; FAT 34 G (INCLUDES 6 G SATURATED FAT); FIBER 13 G

Chicken, Eggplant, and Mint Salad

SERVES 4

SALAD

4 boneless, skinless chicken breast halves (about 5 ounces each)

Salt and pepper

1 tablespoon melted clarified butter

1 eggplant, cut into ½-inch-thick slices

2 scallions, white and green parts, thinly sliced

Large handful of fresh mint leaves

2 tablespoons sunflower seeds, toasted

DRESSING

3 tablespoons fructose powder

2 tablespoons Asian fish sauce

2 garlic cloves, finely chopped

1 green chile pepper, seeded and thinly sliced

Juice of 4 limes

¼ cup olive oil

1 lemongrass stalk, outer layers peeled off, finely chopped (optional)

1 small onion, finely chopped

Eggplant and mint are typical Mediterranean ingredients, but the spicy-salty-sour dressing is inspired by Thai food.

1 Preheat the oven to 250°F or the lowest setting.

2 Heat a ridged grill pan over medium–high heat. Season the chicken breasts with a little salt and pepper, brush with half of the melted butter, then place in the grill pan, and cook until they are seared and patterned with char marks, 3 to 5 minutes per side.

3 Transfer the chicken breasts to a baking dish and place in the oven. Bake until cooked through, 25 to 30 minutes; the juices should run clear when the chicken is pierced with a knife. Set aside to cool until just warm.

4 Meanwhile, wipe out the grill pan and brush with the remaining butter. Add the eggplant slices and cook until tender, 3 to 5 minutes per side. Remove from the pan and set aside to cool.

5 To make the dressing, combine the fructose, fish sauce, garlic, chile, lime juice, and olive oil in a bowl and mix well. Stir in the lemongrass and onion.

6 Cut or tear the cooked chicken into strips and dice the eggplant. Place both in a serving dish with the scallions and pour the dressing on top. Cover and let sit for 30 minutes so the flavors can develop and blend.

7 Sprinkle the mint leaves and toasted sunflower seeds on top and serve.

PER SERVING GLYCEMIC LOAD 4; PROTEIN 36 G; CARBOHYDRATES 26 G; FAT 21 G (INCLUDES 4 G SATURATED FAT); FIBER 5 G

◄ Chicken, Walnut, and Red Bean Salad

SERVES 4

SALAD

1 ripe avocado

1 cup canned red kidney beans, rinsed and drained

3 cups diced cooked chicken

1 small red onion, thinly sliced

Bunch arugula (about 5 ounces)

1 small lollo rosso or other red lettuce, torn into pieces

2 ripe tomatoes, cut into wedges

Scant ½ cup chopped walnuts

DRESSING

Juice of 1 lemon

3 tablespoons olive oil

1 tablespoon balsamic vinegar

1 tablespoon soy sauce

1 tablespoon Dijon mustard

1 teaspoon fructose powder

Salt and pepper

This is a satisfying and versatile main course salad. Instead of lollo rosso you could use baby spinach; instead of red beans, try chickpeas; and if you don't like walnuts, substitute a thinly sliced small leek, which will give a delicate crunch to the salad.

1 Halve the avocado, remove the pit, and peel off the skin. (The easiest way to do this is to use a spoon and insert it just inside the skin; slide the spoon all around to remove the flesh.) Cut the avocado flesh into small dice.

2 Combine the avocado with the beans, chicken, onion, arugula, lettuce, and tomatoes in a salad bowl.

3 To make the dressing, stir together the lemon juice, oil, vinegar, soy sauce, mustard, fructose, and salt and pepper to taste, or shake them in a screwtop jar. Add to the salad and mix together gently. Sprinkle with the walnuts before serving.

PER SERVING GLYCEMIC LOAD 5; PROTEIN 40 G; CARBOHYDRATES 27 G; FAT 32 G (INCLUDES 5 G SATURATED FAT); FIBER 10 G

Tomato Salad with Beans and Basil

SERVES 4

SALAD

1 pound ripe tomatoes, cut into chunks

1 onion, finely chopped

1 15-ounce can black beans or chickpeas, rinsed and drained

DRESSING

Large bunch fresh basil, coarsely chopped

2 garlic cloves, chopped

7 tablespoons olive oil

2 tablespoons balsamic vinegar or white wine vinegar

Pinch of fructose powder, or to taste

Salt and pepper

Serve this with cold ham or turkey to make a satisfying meal. An excellent variation is to scatter a little chopped avocado on top just before serving.

1 Combine the tomatoes, onion, and beans or chickpeas in a salad bowl.

2 To make the dressing, blend the basil, garlic, oil, vinegar, and fructose with a hand-held blender. Alternatively, purée in a food processor. Season with salt and pepper.

3 Pour the dressing over the salad and mix gently but thoroughly. Let sit for 15 to 30 minutes before serving so the flavors can blend.

PER SERVING GLYCEMIC LOAD 6; PROTEIN 9 G; CARBOHYDRATES 31 G; FAT 24 G (INCLUDES 3 G SATURATED FAT); FIBER 10 G

Italian Bean Salad

This main course salad is perfect for a summer buffet.

SERVES 4

SALAD

Bunch arugula (about 5 ounces)

1 10-ounce package frozen artichoke hearts, thawed and cut into small pieces

1 cup canned red kidney beans, rinsed and drained

4 ounces roast turkey breast, cut into strips

4 ounces cooked ham, cut into strips

3 large, ripe tomatoes, diced

4 hard-boiled eggs, quartered

2 tablespoons toasted sunflower seeds

DRESSING

3 tablespoons olive oil

2 tablespoons white wine vinegar

2 garlic cloves, crushed

1 tablespoon chopped fresh oregano or 1 teaspoon dried

2 tablespoons chopped fresh parsley

1 Combine the arugula in a salad bowl with the artichoke hearts, beans, turkey, ham, and tomatoes.

2 To make the dressing, mix together the oil, vinegar, garlic, oregano, and parsley with a hand-held blender or shake them in a screwtop jar.

3 Garnish the salad with the eggs and sprinkle with the sunflower seeds. Pour the dressing over the salad or serve it alongside.

PER SERVING GLYCEMIC LOAD 6; PROTEIN 29 G; CARBOHYDRATES 25 G; FAT 24 G (INCLUDES 5 G SATURATED FAT); FIBER 10 G

White Bean Salad

SERVES 4

SALAD

1¼ cups dried butter beans or other large white beans

1 red or white onion, finely chopped

2 tablespoons finely chopped cornichons

⅔ cup sun-dried tomatoes, cut into thin strips

2 tablespoons chopped fresh chives

DRESSING

5 tablespoons fromage blanc or quark

2 tablespoons reduced-fat crème fraîche or sour cream

1 tablespoon cold-pressed flaxseed oil

Juice of ½ lemon

Chopped fresh herbs such as basil and parsley, to taste

Salt and pepper

A good alternative to potato salad, this goes really well with cured meats. For a spicy kick, add a little finely chopped red chile pepper.

1 Soak the beans in a generous amount of water overnight.

2 Drain the beans and put them into a saucepan with plenty of fresh cold water. Bring to a boil and then simmer until completely soft; this will take about 1 hour. Drain the beans in a colander and then refresh under cold running water. Drain well.

3 Put the beans in a large bowl and add the onion, cornichons, sun-dried tomatoes, and chives.

4 To make the dressing, mix together the fromage blanc, crème fraîche, oil, lemon juice, and herbs and season with salt and pepper.

5 Pour the dressing over the bean mixture and fold everything together. Serve at once.

PER SERVING GLYCEMIC LOAD 10; PROTEIN 7 G; CARBOHYDRATES 22 G; FAT 5 G (INCLUDES 1 G SATURATED FAT); FIBER 5 G

Piquant Pasta Salad with Tuna

SERVES 4

7 ounces dried fusilli pasta (preferably whole-wheat)

1 cucumber

5 tablespoons fromage blanc or quark

Juice of ½ lemon

2 tablespoons chopped fresh dill

1 tablespoon sweet chile sauce

1 tablespoon cold-pressed flaxseed oil (optional)

2 tablespoons chopped cornichons

Salt and pepper

1 12-ounce can tuna in water, drained and flaked

1 pint cherry tomatoes, halved

1 red onion, thinly sliced

1 tablespoon capers

This is a good mid-week meal as it uses mainly pantry staples.

1 Cook the pasta in plenty of lightly salted boiling water until al dente. Drain in a colander and set aside to cool.

2 Peel the cucumber, cut it in half lengthwise and scrape out the seeds with a teaspoon. Cut the cucumber into strips about 2 inches long.

3 Put the fromage blanc in a bowl and add the lemon juice, dill, chile sauce, flaxseed oil, and cornichons. Season with salt and pepper.

4 Combine the pasta, tuna, cucumber, tomatoes, and onion in a large salad bowl. Pour the dressing on top and fold together carefully. Sprinkle the capers over the top.

PER SERVING GLYCEMIC LOAD 14; PROTEIN 31 G; CARBOHYDRATES 47 G; FAT 2 G (INCLUDES 0 G SATURATED FAT); FIBER 6 G

Pesto, Shrimp, and Pasta Salad

SERVES 4

5 ounces dried fusilli pasta (preferably whole-wheat)

1 tablespoon clarified butter

2 celery stalks, diced

1 green bell pepper, seeded and diced

1 red bell pepper, seeded and diced

2 scallions, white and green parts, finely chopped

14 ounces cooked shelled shrimp (thawed if frozen)

½ cup Pesto Sauce (page 86)

A little fresh lemon juice

Unsalted peanuts (optional)

A simple yet incredibly tasty salad.

1 Cook the pasta in plenty of lightly salted boiling water until al dente. Drain in a colander and then rinse with cold running water. Leave the pasta to drain well.

2 Melt the butter in a large skillet over medium heat, add the celery and red and green peppers, and soften slightly without coloring, 3 to 5 minutes. Add the scallions and cook for 1 minute, then remove the vegetables from the pan, and set aside to cool to room temperature.

3 Place the pasta, vegetables, and shrimp in a bowl and mix well. Thin the pesto with a little lemon juice, then pour over the salad, and toss well. Sprinkle a few peanuts on top before serving.

PER SERVING GLYCEMIC LOAD 13; PROTEIN 32 G; CARBOHYDRATES 33 G; FAT 28 G (INCLUDES 8 G SATURATED FAT); FIBER 6 G

Avocado, Zucchini, and Pasta Salad ▶

SERVES 4

PASTA SALAD

9 ounces dried fusilli pasta (preferably whole-wheat)

3 tablespoons olive oil

1 zucchini, halved and sliced

2 ripe avocados

2 tablespoons chopped fresh parsley

Grated zest of 1 lemon

DRESSING

¼ cup olive oil

2 tablespoons white wine vinegar

1 teaspoon Dijon mustard

½ teaspoon fructose powder

2 tablespoons freshly grated Parmesan cheese

1 tablespoon cold-pressed flaxseed oil (optional)

Salt and pepper

Serve with meat or fish. Also good with other dishes as part of a buffet.

1 Cook the pasta in plenty of lightly salted boiling water until al dente. Drain in a colander, then return the pasta to the pot, and add 2 tablespoons of the olive oil, turning the pasta gently to coat with the oil. Set aside to cool.

2 Heat the remaining 1 tablespoon olive oil in a medium skillet over medium heat, add the zucchini, and cook until soft but not brown, 2 to 3 minutes. Remove from the pan and set aside to cool.

3 To make the dressing, mix together the olive oil, vinegar, mustard, fructose, Parmesan, and flaxseed oil. Season with salt and pepper.

4 Halve and pit the avocados. Spoon out the flesh and cut it into pieces.

5 Place the pasta in a large bowl. Add the zucchini, avocado, parsley, lemon zest, and dressing and gently mix everything together.

PER SERVING GLYCEMIC LOAD 18; PROTEIN 11 G; CARBOHYDRATES 57 G; FAT 41 G (INCLUDES 6 G SATURATED FAT); FIBER 13 G

Greek Salad

SERVES 4

A lazy summer day in Greece: lunch al fresco at a taverna by the sea, a glass of chilled white wine, and a Greek salad—life is beautiful.

DRESSING

7 tablespoons olive oil

3 tablespoons white or red wine vinegar

Pinch of dry mustard

Salt and pepper

SALAD

2 heads romaine lettuce

2 large, ripe tomatoes, chopped

1 cucumber, peeled and sliced

1 red onion, thinly sliced

1 green bell pepper, seeded and cut into strips

⅓ cup Kalamata olives

4 ounces diced feta cheese (1 cup)

2 teaspoons chopped fresh oregano or 1 teaspoon dried

1 Make the dressing by combining the olive oil, vinegar, mustard, and a little salt and pepper in a screwtop jar. Shake well. Taste the dressing and add more salt and pepper if necessary.

2 Place the lettuce leaves in a salad bowl or on a platter. Arrange the tomatoes, cucumber, onion, bell pepper, olives, feta, and oregano over the lettuce. Drizzle some of the dressing on top and serve the rest alongside.

PER SERVING GLYCEMIC LOAD 0; PROTEIN 9 G; CARBOHYDRATES 18 G; FAT 34 G (INCLUDES 9 G SATURATED FAT); FIBER 4 G

Cauliflower and Broccoli Salad with Parmesan Dressing

SERVES 4

SALAD

1 head cauliflower (about 1 pound), separated into florets

1 head broccoli (about 1 pound), separated into florets

2 slices lean bacon, thinly sliced crosswise

DRESSING

3 tablespoons olive oil

½ cup finely grated Parmesan cheese

½ teaspoon fructose powder

1 teaspoon finely chopped fresh thyme or ½ teaspoon dried

Salt and pepper

This salad can also be served warm: Make the dressing first, then pour it over the hot vegetables and scatter over the hot bacon.

1 Bring a large pot of lightly salted water to a boil. Drop the cauliflower and broccoli into the pot and cook until slightly softened, 2 minutes. Drain the vegetables in a colander, then refresh with cold running water, and drain well.

2 Fry the bacon in a skillet over medium-high heat until it is crisp, about 5 minutes. Transfer the bacon to a plate lined with paper towels to drain off excess fat and let cool.

3 To make the dressing, combine the oil, Parmesan, fructose, and thyme with a hand-held blender. Season with salt and pepper.

4 Put the cauliflower and broccoli in a serving dish, pour some of the dressing on top, and scatter with the bacon strips. Serve the rest of the dressing alongside.

PER SERVING GLYCEMIC LOAD 0; PROTEIN 11 G; CARBOHYDRATES 14 G; FAT 17 G (INCLUDES 5 G SATURATED FAT); FIBER 6 G

Curried Yogurt Dressing

MAKES 1 CUP; 6 TO 8 SERVINGS

1 teaspoon curry powder

Juice of ½ lemon

1 cup plain yogurt

2 tablespoons olive oil

½-inch piece fresh ginger, finely grated

1 teaspoon fructose powder

½ red chile pepper, finely chopped (optional)

Salt and pepper

This dressing will enliven most salads and goes particularly well with those based on chicken. You can use fromage blanc or quark instead of yogurt, if you prefer. Also try adding some chopped fresh herbs such as cilantro or lemon thyme as a variation.

Stir the curry powder into the lemon juice, then stir in the yogurt, oil, ginger, fructose, and chile, and season with salt and pepper. Leave the dressing in the refrigerator for an hour before using, if possible, to allow the flavors to develop.

TOTAL FOR RECIPE GLYCEMIC LOAD 2; PROTEIN 10 G; CARBOHYDRATES 26 G; FAT 27 G (INCLUDES 4 G SATURATED FAT); FIBER 1 G

Tomato and Cilantro Salsa ▶

2 ripe tomatoes, chopped

1 small red onion, finely chopped

2 garlic cloves, finely chopped

1 teaspoon finely chopped red chile pepper

2 tablespoons chopped fresh cilantro

2 tablespoons extra-virgin olive oil

1 tablespoon balsamic vinegar

1 teaspoon ground cumin (optional)

Salt and pepper

Serve as a first course with other salads and dips, or to accompany grilled or baked fish, chicken, or meat. In the winter, or when you can't get really ripe tomatoes, use canned tomatoes. This salsa will taste even better if left in the refrigerator for a few hours before serving.

Mix together the tomatoes, onion, garlic, chile pepper, cilantro, oil, vinegar, and cumin in a bowl. Season with a little salt and pepper.

TOTAL FOR RECIPE GLYCEMIC LOAD 1; PROTEIN 4 G; CARBOHYDRATES 23 G; FAT 29 G (INCLUDES 4 G SATURATED FAT); FIBER 5 G

Eggplant Purée ▶

1 pound eggplant

1 tablespoon clarified butter

¼ cup finely chopped shallot

1 garlic clove, crushed

1 ripe tomato, peeled, seeded, and diced

1 heaped teaspoon finely chopped fresh parsley

1 heaped teaspoon finely chopped fresh cilantro

3 tablespoons olive oil

2 teaspoons cold-pressed flaxseed oil (optional)

A little fresh lemon juice

Salt and pepper

This can be served warm or at room temperature. Note that the tomatoes must be fresh and ripe—canned will not do here.

1 Preheat the broiler to high.

2 Put the eggplant on a baking sheet and broil, turning to color evenly, until the skin is completely black but not charred, 10 to 15 minutes. (Alternatively, you can do this over a gas burner, with the eggplant pierced on a long-handled metal fork.) Set aside to cool. When cool enough to handle, peel off the skin and chop the flesh very finely. Place the eggplant flesh in a bowl.

3 Melt the butter in a skillet, add the shallot and garlic, and cook until the shallot is softened but not browned, 3 minutes. Add the tomato, parsley, and cilantro. Cook for 2 minutes to allow the flavors to develop.

4 Spoon the tomato and shallot mixture into the bowl with the eggplant. Add the olive and flaxseed oils and lemon juice and mix together. Season with salt and pepper.

TOTAL FOR RECIPE GLYCEMIC LOAD 1; PROTEIN 8 G; CARBOHYDRATES 42 G; FAT 53 G (INCLUDES 13 G SATURATED FAT); FIBER 18 G

Pesto Sauce

MAKES 1 CUP; 6 TO 8 SERVINGS

3 tablespoons pine nuts

1¼ cups fresh basil leaves

2 garlic cloves, crushed

½ cup freshly grated Parmesan cheese

¼ cup olive oil

Salt and pepper

This makes a thick pesto. For a thinner consistency, to make a sauce that can be used as a salad dressing, adjust the quantity of oil.

1 Toast the pine nuts lightly in a dry skillet over medium heat until just golden but not browned, 5 minutes. Set aside to cool.

2 Put the pine nuts in a food processor or blender, add the basil, garlic, Parmesan, and oil, and purée to make a smooth sauce. Season with salt and pepper.

TOTAL FOR RECIPE GLYCEMIC LOAD 0; PROTEIN 22 G; CARBOHYDRATES 8 G; FAT 91 G (INCLUDES 23 G SATURATED FAT); FIBER 4 G

Mustard and Basil Dressing

MAKES 1 CUP; 8 TO 10 SERVINGS

¾ cup olive oil

1¼ cups fresh basil leaves

3 garlic cloves, finely chopped

2 tablespoons coarse-grain mustard

Salt and pepper

Pinch of fructose powder, or to taste

Instead of basil, you can use tarragon or oregano in this flavorful salad dressing.

Combine the oil, basil, garlic, and mustard in a food processor and purée until smooth. Season with salt, pepper, and fructose. Let sit for 15 minutes before using, to allow the flavors to develop.

TOTAL FOR RECIPE GLYCEMIC LOAD 0; PROTEIN 4 G; CARBOHYDRATES 10 G; FAT 165 G (INCLUDES 22 G SATURATED FAT); FIBER 3 G

Avocado Dip

MAKES 1¼ CUPS; 2 TO 4 SERVINGS

2 ripe avocados

Juice of ½ lemon

5 tablespoons fromage blanc

¼ small red chile pepper, seeded and finely chopped

2 garlic cloves, finely chopped

1 shallot, finely chopped

Salt and pepper

Pinch of fructose powder, or to taste

Serve as a first course or snack, with sticks of raw vegetables.

1 Halve and pit the avocados. Scoop out the flesh, put it in a bowl, and mash it with a fork. It doesn't need to be completely smooth. Mix in the lemon juice.

2 Add the fromage blanc, chile, garlic, and shallot and mix well. Season with salt, pepper, and fructose.

TOTAL FOR RECIPE GLYCEMIC LOAD 2; PROTEIN 15 G; CARBOHYDRATES 42 G; FAT 59 G (INCLUDES 9 G SATURATED FAT); FIBER 27 G

Hummus

MAKES 2 CUPS: 6 TO 8 SERVINGS

1 15-ounce can chickpeas,
rinsed and drained

Scant ½ cup tahini

2 garlic cloves, crushed

3 tablespoons olive oil

Juice of 1 lemon

Salt and pepper

1 teaspoon paprika, for garnish

Chopped fresh parsley, for garnish

Set the bowl of hummus in the middle of a large dish and arrange sticks of raw vegetables neatly around it—perfect for a snack. Hummus can also be spread on bread in place of butter.

1 Place the chickpeas in a food processor or blender and process to a coarse paste.

2 Stir the tahini with 1 to 2 tablespoons water, then add to the food processor along with the garlic, and process to mix. With the machine running, slowly add the olive oil and lemon juice through the hole in the lid and process to a smooth paste. Season with salt and pepper.

3 Transfer to a serving bowl and sprinkle with the paprika and parsley.

TOTAL FOR RECIPE GLYCEMIC LOAD 18; PROTEIN 48 G; CARBOHYDRATES 120 G; FAT 105 G (INCLUDES 14 G SATURATED FAT); FIBER 31 G

Tzatziki

MAKES 3 CUPS: 6 TO 8 SERVINGS

1 pound thick, Greek-style yogurt
or plain yogurt

2 cucumbers

Salt and pepper

3 garlic cloves, finely chopped

3 tablespoons olive oil

A little fresh lemon juice

Pinch of fructose powder,
or to taste

This classic Greek cucumber and yogurt salad (illustrated on page 85) is good as an accompaniment to grilled fish, or as a dip with raw mixed vegetables.

1 If using plain yogurt, put the yogurt in a sieve lined with a coffee filter or cheesecloth and set over a bowl. Leave to drain for at least 2 hours, or, ideally, overnight in the refrigerator. (This isn't necessary if you use Greek-style yogurt, as it has already been drained.)

2 Peel the cucumbers and halve lengthwise. Scrape out the seeds with a teaspoon. Coarsely grate the cucumber and mix with a little salt in a bowl. Let sit for 10 to 15 minutes, and then squeeze out as much liquid from the cucumber as possible.

3 Add the garlic to the yogurt, along with the oil. Mix in the cucumber and season with lemon juice, fructose, salt, and pepper.

TOTAL FOR RECIPE GLYCEMIC LOAD 11; PROTEIN 39 G; CARBOHYDRATES 30 G; FAT 50 G (INCLUDES 12 G SATURATED FAT); FIBER 3 G

Mussels with White Beans and Olives

SERVES 4

1½ cups dried white beans

2 pounds mussels in their shells

4 tablespoons clarified butter

½ onion, finely chopped

Salt and pepper

¾ cup dry white wine

2 garlic cloves, finely chopped

1 15-ounce can chopped tomatoes

1 tablespoon finely chopped fresh cilantro

2 tablespoons fresh lemon juice

8 pitted black olives, halved

¼ teaspoon fructose powder

2 tablespoons chopped fresh parsley

You will love this hearty stew—it is tasty and filling, with just the right balance of sweet, sour, and salty flavors.

1 Soak the beans in a generous amount of water overnight.

2 Drain the beans and put them in a large saucepan with plenty of fresh cold water. Bring to a boil, then reduce the heat, and simmer until soft, about 1½ hours. Drain well.

3 Clean the mussels thoroughly in cold water. Discard any mussels that are damaged or that do not close when tapped.

4 Melt 2 tablespoons of the butter in a large saucepan over medium heat. Add the onion and a little pepper and cook for 1 minute. Add the mussels and ½ cup of the wine. Put on the lid and cook until the mussels open, 3 to 5 minutes. Drain the mussels, reserving the cooking liquid. Discard any mussels that have not opened. Shell the mussels, reserving some in their shells for garnish. Cover the mussels to keep them warm.

5 Melt the remaining 2 tablespoons butter in a medium saucepan over medium heat. Add the garlic and cook for 1 to 2 minutes. Add the tomatoes, cilantro, the remaining ¼ cup wine, the lemon juice, and olives. Simmer for 5 minutes. Add the beans, mussels, and their cooking liquid. Place over low heat to heat everything through. Season to taste with salt, pepper, and fructose. Sprinkle with parsley and serve at once.

PER SERVING GLYCEMIC LOAD 5; PROTEIN 25 G; CARBOHYDRATES 59 G; FAT 16 G (INCLUDES 8 G SATURATED FAT); FIBER 20 G

Grilled Squid Stuffed with Feta Cheese

SERVES 4

4 large squid (about
8 ounces each)

4-ounce block feta cheese

Scant ½ cup olive oil, plus extra
for brushing

2 garlic cloves, crushed

4 fresh marjoram leaves,
finely chopped

Salt and pepper

Lemon wedges, for garnish

An unusual but simple dish for a summer barbecue. Serve with Tomato Salad with Beans and Basil (page 77) or with Herbed Quinoa Pilaf (page 144).

1 To clean the squid: Pull the tentacles gently away from the body. Discard the innards and the hard "quill." Trim off and discard the hard part at the top of the tentacles, leaving the tentacles joined together. Rinse thoroughly and dry with paper towels.

2 Cut the feta into 8 pieces, each ½ x ½ x 2 inches.

3 Put the squid and feta cheese in a glass dish just large enough to hold them all side by side. Mix together the olive oil, garlic, and marjoram; season to taste with salt and pepper. Pour over the squid and cheese, cover the dish, and refrigerate for 2 to 3 hours.

4 Gently push 2 sticks of feta cheese into each squid body. Spear the tentacles onto a skewer.

5 Preheat the grill to high or heat a ridged grill pan over high heat. Brush the grill rack or pan with olive oil, then add the squid bodies, and grill for about 5 minutes. Carefully turn the squid over and grill for 2 minutes. Grill the tentacles for 2 minutes per side. Serve at once, with lemon wedges.

PER SERVING GLYCEMIC LOAD 0; PROTEIN 39 G; CARBOHYDRATES 8 G; FAT 32 G (INCLUDES 8 G SATURATED FAT); FIBER 0 G

Squid with Fennel and Spinach

SERVES 6

2 to 2½ pounds squid

Scant ½ cup olive oil

1 onion, finely chopped

2 fennel bulbs, sliced

3 cups chopped fresh spinach

2 scallions, white and green parts, sliced

2 ripe tomatoes, diced

Salt and pepper

Juice of 1 large lemon

If you are short of time, use frozen calamari rings instead of fresh squid.

1 To clean the squid: Pull the tentacles gently away from the body. Discard the innards and the hard "quill." Trim off and discard the hard part at the top of the tentacles, leaving the tentacles joined together. Rinse the squid thoroughly, pat dry, and chop into bite-sized pieces.

2 Heat the oil in a large, heavy saucepan over medium heat. Add the onion and cook for 2 minutes. Add the squid and cook, stirring, until the squid becomes opaque, about 2 minutes. Add a scant 2 cups water, cover with a lid, and simmer over low heat for 45 minutes.

3 Add the fennel, spinach, scallions, and tomatoes, season with salt and pepper, and mix well. Add more water if the pan is dry. Cover and cook until the fennel is tender, 5 to 10 minutes. Remove from the heat, add the lemon juice and let sit for 10 to 15 minutes before serving.

PER SERVING GLYCEMIC LOAD 0; PROTEIN 26 G; CARBOHYDRATES 17 G; FAT 18 G (INCLUDES 3 G SATURATED FAT); FIBER 4 G

Mussel and Mushroom Fricassée

SERVES 4

4 pounds mussels in their shells

2 tablespoons clarified butter

3 tablespoons dry white wine (optional)

1½ cups chicken broth

6 tablespoons half-and-half

1 pound button mushrooms, sliced

Salt and pepper

2 bunches arugula (about 8 ounces), coarsely chopped

1 teaspoon chopped fresh tarragon

1 small bunch chives, chopped

1 tablespoon capers

For a healthy lunch or supper, accompany with a bean or lentil salad.

1 Clean the mussels thoroughly in cold water. Discard any mussels that are damaged or that do not close when tapped.

2 Melt 1 tablespoon of the butter in a large saucepan over medium-high heat. Add the mussels and cover the pan. When the mussels start to open, about 3 minutes, pour in the white wine and broth and cook until the mussels have opened, 2 to 3 minutes. Strain the broth into a clean saucepan. Shell the mussels.

3 Add the half-and-half to the mussel broth and simmer over medium heat to concentrate the flavor and thicken the sauce, 5 to 10 minutes.

4 Meanwhile, melt the remaining tablespoon butter in a large skillet over medium-high heat. Add the mushrooms and cook until golden, 5 to 10 minutes. Season with plenty of pepper.

5 Mix the mushrooms, mussels, arugula, and tarragon into the sauce. Taste and season with salt if necessary. Sprinkle with chives and capers and serve at once.

PER SERVING GLYCEMIC LOAD 0; PROTEIN 23 G; CARBOHYDRATES 10 G; FAT 12 G (INCLUDES 6 G SATURATED FAT); FIBER 2 G

Baked Shrimp with Tomatoes and Feta

In Greece—where this dish is called saganáki—*the shrimp are cooked in their shells (which keeps them tender and juicy) and served warm rather than finger-burning hot. This recipe stays true to the original in that respect; however, if you don't want to eat the shrimp with your fingers, peel them before you cook them, leaving the tails on if you like.*

SERVES 4

1 pound shell-on large shrimp

4 tablespoons olive oil

4 large shallots, finely sliced

4 garlic cloves, crushed

3 tablespoons fresh thyme leaves or 1½ tablespoons dried

2 bay leaves

1 cinnamon stick or ½ teaspoon ground cinnamon

1¾ pounds ripe tomatoes, peeled, seeded, and chopped

Salt and pepper

9 ounces feta cheese, crumbled (2¼ cups)

1 bunch scallions, white and green parts, finely chopped

½ teaspoon fennel seeds

2 teaspoons cold-pressed flaxseed oil (optional)

1 Preheat the oven to 350°F.

2 Heat 2 tablespoons of the olive oil in a sauté pan over low heat, add the shallots and cook until soft, 5 minutes. Add 1 of the garlic cloves, 2 tablespoons of the thyme, the bay leaves, and cinnamon. Add the tomatoes, stir briefly, then cover, and simmer for 5 to 10 minutes, to allow the flavors to blend. Season to taste with salt and pepper.

3 Transfer the tomato sauce to a large, shallow ovenproof dish. Sprinkle the feta cheese on top and place in the oven for about 5 minutes.

4 Meanwhile, heat 1 tablespoon of the oil in a large skillet over medium heat. Add the scallions and the remaining 3 garlic cloves, and 1 tablespoon thyme and sauté for 1 to 2 minutes. Add the shrimp and fennel seeds and cook, turning frequently, until the shrimp are opaque, about 2 minutes. Add the shrimp to the dish with the tomatoes and feta and return the dish to the oven for 10 minutes so the flavors can develop fully.

5 Drizzle the remaining tablespoon of olive oil over the top, together with the flaxseed oil, if using. Leave to cool slightly before serving.

PER SERVING GLYCEMIC LOAD 0; PROTEIN 20 G; CARBOHYDRATES 26 G; FAT 28 G (INCLUDES 12 G SATURATED FAT); FIBER 5 G

Marinated Shrimp

SERVES 4

Scant ½ cup olive oil
½ red onion, finely chopped
3 garlic cloves, finely chopped
½ small red chile pepper,
seeded and finely chopped
1 tablespoon chopped
fresh cilantro
8 black olives,
pitted and chopped
Juice of 1 lime
Salt and pepper
1 pound shelled cooked shrimp

This dish can be eaten with a slice of good bread for breakfast or brunch, in a salad for lunch, or as a first course for dinner. It's a good alternative to a shrimp cocktail.

Mix together the oil, onion, garlic, chile pepper, cilantro, olives, lime juice, and salt and pepper to taste. Add the shrimp and stir well. Cover and chill for at least 1 hour or overnight before serving.

PER SERVING GLYCEMIC LOAD 0; PROTEIN 29 G; CARBOHYDRATES 4 G; FAT 28 G (INCLUDES 3.5 G SATURATED FAT); FIBER 0.5 G

MAKE AHEAD If you wish, you can marinate the shrimp up to a day ahead.

Salmon Fishcakes

SERVES 4

1 pound salmon fillet
¾ cup half-and-half
2 ounces smoked salmon,
finely chopped
1 shallot, finely chopped
1 tablespoon chopped fresh dill
1 large egg
Salt and pepper
1 tablespoon clarified butter

Instead of salmon, you could use a less expensive white fish to make these delicate fishcakes. Serve them with salad, green lentils, or Mung Bean and Tomato salad (page 142).

1 Remove the skin from the salmon and run your fingers over the flesh to check that there are no bones; if you find any, use tweezers to pull them out. Put the salmon in a food processor and pulse to chop coarsely.

2 Add the half-and-half, smoked salmon, shallot, dill, and egg to the food processor and process for 10 to 15 seconds, until you have an even, relatively coarse paste that holds together. Season with salt and pepper.

3 Melt the butter in a nonstick skillet over medium heat. Divide the salmon mixture into 8 and shape into 1-inch-thick cakes. Cook, turning carefully, until golden on both sides, 3 to 5 minutes per side. Serve hot.

PER SERVING GLYCEMIC LOAD 0; PROTEIN 28 G; CARBOHYDRATES 2 G; FAT 22 G (INCLUDES 8 G SATURATED FAT); FIBER 0 G

MAKE AHEAD The fishcakes can be prepared a day ahead and kept in the refrigerator before cooking. Alternatively, make double quantities, cook all the fishcakes, and freeze what you don't use.

Seared Salmon with Spicy Pasta

SERVES 4

14 ounces boneless, skinless
salmon fillet

Salt and pepper

2 tablespoons clarified butter

1 onion, finely chopped

1 garlic clove, finely chopped

1 small red chile pepper, seeded
and finely chopped

4 ripe tomatoes, diced

1 teaspoon chili powder

¾ cup half-and-half

7 ounces dried fusilli pasta
(preferably whole-wheat)

1 tablespoon chopped fresh basil

2 tablespoons chopped
fresh parsley

1 tablespoon cold-pressed
flaxseed oil (optional)

Cooked slowly in the oven, this salmon is incredibly moist and improved only by its pasta with spicy tomato sauce accompaniment.

1 Preheat the oven to 250°F or the lowest setting.

2 Place the salmon in an ovenproof dish or a small roasting pan. Season with a little pepper. If you have a roasting thermometer, insert it in the thickest part of the fish. Place the salmon in the oven and cook for 25 to 30 minutes. The core temperature should be 140°F.

3 While the fish is in the oven, melt 1 tablespoon of the butter in a large saucepan over medium heat. Add the onion, garlic, and chile and cook until the vegetables are soft, 5 minutes. Add the tomatoes and cook for 2 minutes. Add the chili powder and then the half-and-half. Cook over low heat for 5 minutes.

4 Meanwhile, cook the pasta in plenty of lightly salted water until al dente. Drain the pasta in a colander.

5 Add the pasta, basil, and parsley to the tomato mixture, mix well, and heat through. Season with salt and a little pepper, to taste. Add the flaxseed oil, if using. Cut the salmon into 4 portions and serve with the spicy pasta.

PER SERVING GLYCEMIC LOAD 14; PROTEIN 29 G; CARBOHYDRATES 50 G; FAT 23 G (INCLUDES 9 G SATURATED FAT); FIBER 7 G

Lemon-Marinated Sardines

SERVES 4

2 to 2½ pounds fresh sardines, scaled and filleted
Salt and white pepper
2 tablespoons chopped fresh cilantro
⅔ cup olive oil
Juice of 4 lemons

In this dish, the sardines are "cooked" by the lemon juice. To make life easier, ask your fishmonger to fillet the sardines.

1 Rinse the sardine fillets and pat dry with paper towels. Place in a glass dish, sprinkle with salt, then cover the dish, and refrigerate for 24 hours.

2 Rinse the fillets to remove excess salt, then pat dry thoroughly with paper towels. Place the sardines in a clean glass dish, then sprinkle with pepper and the cilantro, and pour the olive oil and lemon juice over the top. Cover and refrigerate for 24 to 48 hours before serving.

PER SERVING GLYCEMIC LOAD 0; PROTEIN 56 G; CARBOHYDRATES 4 G; FAT 64 G (INCLUDES 11 G SATURATED FAT); FIBER 0 G

 MAKE AHEAD These sardines need to be started at least 48 hours before being served.

Grilled Sardines ▶

SERVES 4

2 to 2½ pounds fresh sardines, scaled and gutted
6 tablespoons olive oil
Juice of 2 large lemons
1½ tablespoons dried oregano
1 or 2 lemons, quartered, for garnish

This recipe is just as good with other fish—sea bream, small sea bass, or red mullet. A fish weighing about 10 to 12 ounces will serve one person. Greek Salad (page 82) would be a good accompaniment, along with delicious Almond and Garlic Sauce (page 104).

1 Rinse the sardines and pat dry with paper towels. Cut 3 shallow slits on each side.

2 Preheat the grill to high and oil the grill rack.

3 Mix the olive oil, lemon juice, and oregano in a small bowl. Brush each fish generously inside and out with the mixture.

4 Grill the sardines, basting with more herbed oil as they cook, until just cooked through, 3 to 4 minutes per side.

5 Serve immediately, with the lemon quarters.

PER SERVING GLYCEMIC LOAD 0; PROTEIN 56 G; CARBOHYDRATES 3 G; FAT 48 G (INCLUDES 9 G SATURATED FAT); FIBER 0 G

Baked Mackerel with Tomatoes and Garlic

SERVES 4

4 medium mackerel,
scaled and gutted

½ tablespoon clarified butter

1 tablespoon olive oil

1 onion, finely chopped

3 garlic cloves, finely chopped

4 ripe tomatoes,
finely chopped

2 tablespoons chopped
fresh parsley

1 tablespoon fructose powder

Salt and pepper

*Frozen mackerel fillets also work well and make it even easier to
prepare this traditional Greek dish.*

1 Preheat the oven to 275°F.

2 Rinse the fish and pat dry. Melt the butter in a large skillet over medium-high heat. Add the fish and brown on both sides, 3 minutes per side.

3 Meanwhile, heat the olive oil in a small saucepan and add the onion and garlic. Cook over medium heat until the onion is translucent, 3 to 5 minutes. Add the tomatoes, parsley, and fructose. Cook for 3 to 4 minutes and then season with salt and pepper.

4 Place the mackerel in a baking dish and pour the tomato sauce on top. Bake for about 40 minutes; turn the fish over a couple of times or spoon over some of the sauce during the cooking period. The fish is done when the flesh flakes easily when pressed with a fork. Serve hot.

PER SERVING GLYCEMIC LOAD 0; PROTEIN 21 G; CARBOHYDRATES 13 G; FAT 7 G
(INCLUDES 2 G SATURATED FAT); FIBER 2 G

Swordfish with Walnut and Garlic Sauce

SERVES 4

½ cup chopped walnuts

1 to 2 garlic cloves,
to taste, crushed

½ cup freshly grated Parmesan
cheese

5 tablespoons chopped fresh
parsley or cilantro

Salt and pepper

2 tablespoons olive oil

½ tablespoon fresh lemon juice

2 tablespoons skim milk

4 swordfish steaks (about
6 ounces each)

1 tablespoon clarified butter

*This is good served with steamed green beans or with legumes such as
green lentils, chickpeas, or butter beans.*

1 Use a food processor or mortar and pestle to make the sauce. Process or grind together the walnuts and garlic until very fine and slightly oily. This will take around 1 minute in a food processor or 6 minutes with a pestle and mortar.

2 Add the Parmesan, parsley, and a little pepper. Process or grind until the mixture forms a smooth paste. Gradually add the olive oil, lemon juice, and milk. Season with salt and pepper to taste.

3 Melt the butter in a large skillet over medium-high heat. Add the swordfish steaks and brown until just cooked through, 3 to 5 minutes per side; do not overcook or the fish will become tough and dry.

4 Serve at once on warmed plates, with a good spoonful of the sauce on each piece of fish.

PER SERVING GLYCEMIC LOAD 0; PROTEIN 38 G; CARBOHYDRATES 3 G; FAT 31 G
(INCLUDES 8 G SATURATED FAT); FIBER 1 G

Red Snapper with Chickpeas, Tomatoes, and Basil

SERVES 4

4 red snapper fillets (10 to 12 ounces each)

3 tablespoons olive oil

3 shallots, chopped

2 15-ounce cans chickpeas, rinsed and drained

2 15-ounce cans chopped tomatoes

2 teaspoons tomato paste

1 teaspoon balsamic vinegar

1 tablespoon chopped fresh thyme

½ teaspoon fructose powder

Salt and pepper

3 tablespoons chopped fresh basil

2 tablespoons chopped fresh parsley

There's nothing quite like the wonderful aromas of fresh basil and thyme to enliven mild white fish such as red snapper.

1 Rinse the fish fillets and dry them well with paper towels. Check that there are no little bones remaining; if you find any, pull them out with tweezers.

2 Heat 2 tablespoons of the olive oil in a large saucepan over medium heat. Add the shallots and chickpeas and cook for 2 to 3 minutes. Add the tomatoes with their juice and the tomato paste. Bring to a boil, then reduce the heat, and simmer for 5 minutes.

3 Stir in the balsamic vinegar, thyme, and fructose, and season with salt and pepper. Simmer gently for 4 to 5 minutes.

4 Meanwhile, heat the remaining tablespoon olive oil in a nonstick skillet, then add the fish, and cook over medium heat, turning carefully, until cooked through, 3 to 5 minutes per side.

5 Stir the basil into the tomato mixture and then divide the mixture between 4 warmed soup plates. Place the fish on top, sprinkle with the parsley, and serve hot.

PER SERVING GLYCEMIC LOAD 8; PROTEIN 76 G; CARBOHYDRATES 67 G; FAT 19 G (INCLUDES 3 G SATURATED FAT); FIBER 18 G

Red Mullet with Orange, Ginger, and Cilantro sauce

SERVES 4

8 small or 4 large red mullet fillets
1 cup fresh orange juice
½ cup olive oil
1 teaspoon grated fresh ginger
1 teaspoon ground cumin
¼ cup finely chopped
fresh cilantro
Salt and pepper
1 tablespoon clarified butter
or olive oil

Serve red mullet skin-side up to appreciate its lovely rich color. Steamed green beans, zucchini, or fennel provide a contrast in color and texture.

1 Run your fingers over the fish fillets to check that no bones remain; if you find any, pull them out with tweezers. Rinse and pat dry the fish.

2 In a large glass dish, mix together the orange juice, olive oil, ginger, cumin, and half of the cilantro. Season with salt and pepper. Add the fish, turn to coat, and refrigerate for 2 hours.

3 Heat the butter in a nonstick skillet over medium heat. Take the fish out of the marinade and add to the pan, turning carefully to cook on both sides, until just cooked through, 2 to 5 minutes.

4 Transfer the fish to warmed plates and wipe the pan clean with paper towels. Pour the marinade into the pan and simmer over medium heat until it begins to thicken, a minute or two. Pour the sauce around the fish and sprinkle with the remaining cilantro.

PER SERVING GLYCEMIC LOAD 0; PROTEIN 16 G; CARBOHYDRATES 7 G; FAT 33 G (INCLUDES 6 G SATURATED FAT); FIBER 0 G

Hake with Red and Green Peppers

SERVES 4

¼ cup chopped fresh parsley

¼ cup olive oil

2 garlic cloves

1 small red chile pepper, seeded and finely chopped

½ red bell pepper, finely chopped

½ green bell pepper, finely chopped

2 ripe tomatoes, peeled and diced

1 teaspoon fructose powder

1 tablespoon balsamic vinegar

Salt and pepper

1¾ pounds hake fillet

½ cup finely grated Parmesan cheese

Almost any kind of fish could be used for this recipe. Tzatziki (page 87) is a good accompaniment or serve with a simple vegetable dish, plus a dish of beans, lentils, or chickpeas.

1 Preheat the oven to 250°F or the lowest setting.

2 To make the topping mix together the parsley, oil, chile pepper, red and green bell peppers, tomatoes, fructose, vinegar, and salt and pepper to taste.

3 Run your fingers over the fish to check that there are no bones; if you find any, pull them out with tweezers. Rinse and pat dry the fillets. Cut the fish into 4 portions and place in a baking dish.

4 Spread the topping over the fish and sprinkle the Parmesan on top. Bake until the fish is cooked through, about 30 minutes. Serve hot.

PER SERVING GLYCEMIC LOAD 0; PROTEIN 43 G; CARBOHYDRATES 7 G; FAT 30 G (INCLUDES 7 G SATURATED FAT); FIBER 1.5 G

Cod with Pesto

SERVES 4

1¾ pounds cod fillet

¼ cup pesto sauce, homemade (page 86) or store-bought

Pepper

You could use almost any filleted fish in this simple, tasty recipe: Try it with sea bass or other mild fish. Cooking at a low temperature keeps the fish moist and tender.

1 Preheat the oven to 250°F or the lowest setting.

2 Remove the skin from the fish and run your fingers over the flesh to check that there are no bones; if you find any, pull them out with tweezers. Rinse and pat dry the fish.

3 Put the fish in a lightly oiled baking dish in one layer. Spread the pesto over the fish and sprinkle with pepper. Bake until the fish is cooked through, about 30 minutes. Cut into 4 portions and serve hot.

PER SERVING GLYCEMIC LOAD 0; PROTEIN 38 G; CARBOHYDRATES 1 G; FAT 8 G (INCLUDES 2 G SATURATED FAT); FIBER 0 G

Monkfish with Herbed Olive Oil

SERVES 4

Scant ½ cup olive oil

¼ cup chopped fresh herbs, such as basil, thyme, or parsley

2 tablespoons freshly grated Parmesan cheese

1 tablespoon fresh lemon juice

Salt and pepper

1¾ pounds monkfish fillet

This easy, flavorful recipe works just as well with flat fish such as sole or flounder, or with less expensive white fish.

1 Preheat the oven to 250°F or the lowest setting.

2 Combine the oil, herbs, Parmesan, lemon juice, and salt and pepper to taste in a blender or food processor. Process the mixture until it is fairly smooth and thick.

3 Cut the fish into 4 portions and place in a baking dish. Spoon the herbed oil over the fish to coat well. (Note—you may not need all the oil: It can be served as a sauce on the side or reserved for another use. Store in an airtight jar in the refrigerator.)

4 Place the fish in the oven. Bake until the fish is cooked through, about 30 minutes. Serve hot.

PER SERVING GLYCEMIC LOAD 0; PROTEIN 30 G; CARBOHYDRATES 0 G; FAT 28 G (INCLUDES 5 G SATURATED FAT); FIBER 0 G

Grilled Chicken with Almond and Garlic Sauce

SERVES 4

SAUCE

9 ounces dried large white beans, such as lima beans

½ cup ground almonds

2 garlic cloves

1 tablespoon white wine vinegar

Scant ½ cup olive oil

1 tablespoon fresh lemon juice

1 teaspoon cold-pressed flaxseed oil

½ teaspoon salt

½ teaspoon ground white pepper

CHICKEN

2 spring chickens (poussins), (about 2 pounds each)

Juice of 1 lemon

3 tablespoons olive oil

½ tablespoon dried oregano

3 tablespoons dry white wine

2 garlic cloves, finely chopped

1 onion, finely chopped

Salt and pepper

2 tablespoons chopped fresh herbs, such as parsley, thyme, or oregano

Lemon wedges, to serve

For the best flavor, marinate the chicken overnight. If you're short of time, use a 15-ounce can of cannellini or lima beans instead of the dried beans. With this rich, garlicky sauce, you only need a fresh salad to complete the meal.

1 For the sauce, soak the beans in a generous amount of water overnight.

2 Using poultry shears, cut each chicken along the backbone and remove as much of the backbone as possible. Press the chickens with your fist to flatten slightly and then place them in a large glass dish that will fit in the refrigerator.

3 Combine the lemon juice, olive oil, oregano, wine, garlic, onion, and some salt and pepper in a blender and purée to make a paste. Spread the paste over the chicken and massage it into the meat. Cover the dish and refrigerate for at least 2 hours, or, preferably, overnight.

4 The next day, drain the beans, put them in a saucepan, and add enough fresh water to cover the beans by about 3 inches. Bring to a boil over medium heat and cook for 10 minutes, then reduce the heat, and simmer the beans until completely soft, 1 to 1½ hours,. Drain well.

5 Put the beans, almonds, garlic, and vinegar in a food processor and process to a smooth paste. Gradually add the olive oil and lemon juice through the hole in the lid, processing to a thick sauce. Add the flaxseed oil and season with the salt and pepper. Set aside.

6 Preheat the broiler until very hot, prepare the grill, or preheat the oven to 350°F.

7 Wipe away excess marinade from the chicken, then cook under the broiler, on the barbecue or in a roasting pan in the oven until cooked through, approximately 45 minutes. Test by piercing the thickest part of the flesh with a knife: When the chicken is cooked the juices will run clear.

8 Cut the chickens in half, sprinkle with the herbs, and serve with the sauce and lemon wedges.

PER SERVING GLYCEMIC LOAD 0; PROTEIN 76 G; CARBOHYDRATES 24 G; FAT 45 G (INCLUDES 6 G SATURATED FAT); FIBER 6 G

 MAKE AHEAD The sauce can be made up to 3 days ahead; store in the refrigerator. Serve cool or at room temperature.

Spanish Chicken Casserole with Green Lentils

SERVES 4

7 ounces green lentils

1 tablespoon olive oil

1 tablespoon clarified butter

4 boneless, skinless chicken breast halves, cut into ¾-inch cubes

1 small onion, finely chopped

1 green bell pepper, seeded and diced

2 celery stalks, finely diced

1 15-ounce can chopped tomatoes

1¾ cups chicken broth

2 garlic cloves, crushed

1 teaspoon ground cumin

Pinch of cayenne pepper, or to taste

Salt and pepper

1 tablespoon cold-pressed flaxseed oil

2 tablespoons chopped fresh parsley

This is a delicious casserole rich with heart-healthy oils and the wonderful scent of cumin.

1 Put the lentils in a saucepan and cover with plenty of water. Bring to a boil, then lower the heat, and simmer until soft, about 30 minutes. Drain well, then mix with the olive oil, and keep hot.

2 Meanwhile, melt the butter in a large saucepan over medium heat. Add the chicken and cook, turning the pieces so they color evenly, until browned, 4 to 5 minutes. Transfer to a plate.

3 Lower the heat slightly and add the onion, green pepper, and celery to the pan. Cook until the vegetables start to soften, about 4 minutes. Stir in the tomatoes and broth. Simmer gently for 10 to 12 minutes.

4 Add the garlic, cumin, and cayenne pepper to the tomato sauce. Season with salt and pepper, if necessary. Return the chicken to the sauce and simmer until cooked through, about 10 minutes.

5 Place the hot lentils in a serving dish and gently mix in the chicken and sauce. Sprinkle with the flaxseed oil and parsley and serve hot.

PER SERVING GLYCEMIC LOAD 2; PROTEIN 46 G; CARBOHYDRATES 41 G; FAT 13 G (INCLUDES 3 G SATURATED FAT); FIBER 10 G

Chicken Baked in Spiced Yogurt

SERVES 6

6 skinless chicken legs or
6 thighs and 6 drumsticks
½ cup plain yogurt
½ cup olive oil
Juice of 1 lemon
2 garlic cloves, crushed
1 teaspoon paprika
A good pinch of ground cinnamon
Pinch of cayenne pepper
Salt and pepper
1 tablespoon clarified butter
Lemon wedges, to serve

These chicken legs make an easy supper dish, but are just as good cold for a summer lunch. Serve with a bean or lentil dish and a mixed salad.

1 If using chicken legs, divide each leg into thighs and drumsticks, cutting at the joint.

2 Mix together the yogurt, olive oil, lemon juice, garlic, paprika, cinnamon, cayenne pepper, and some salt and pepper in a resealable plastic bag. Add the chicken pieces and seal the bag. Squeeze the bag gently to distribute the marinade all over the chicken. Leave in the refrigerator for at least 2 to 3 hours or, preferably, overnight.

3 Preheat the oven to 250°F or the lowest setting.

4 Melt the butter in a large skillet over medium-high heat. Add the chicken and its marinade and brown the chicken pieces on all sides, 5 to 7 minutes. Transfer them to a roasting pan and finish cooking in the oven until cooked through, 40 to 50 minutes. If you are using a roasting thermometer, insert it into the thickest part of a thigh and set the temperature to 150°F. Otherwise test for doneness by piercing the chicken with a knife: When the chicken is cooked, the juices will run clear.

5 Serve the chicken hot or cold, with lemon wedges.

PER SERVING GLYCEMIC LOAD 0; PROTEIN 27 G; CARBOHYDRATES 2 G; FAT 25 G (INCLUDES 5 G SATURATED FAT); FIBER 0.5 G

MAKE AHEAD The chicken is best when marinated overnight. If you want to serve it cold, it can be cooked a day or two ahead and stored in the refrigerator.

Greek Chicken with Artichokes and Tomato Avgolemono

SERVES 4

1 chicken (about 3½ pounds), skinned and cut into 4 or 8 pieces

Salt and pepper

3 tablespoons olive oil

1 large red onion, finely chopped

2 garlic cloves, finely chopped

1 tablespoon tomato paste

3 lemons

¾ cup brandy or dry white wine

1 teaspoon ground cinnamon

4 fresh, frozen (thawed) or canned (rinsed) artichoke hearts

2 eggs

⅓ cup pine nuts, lightly toasted

Avgolemono is a classic Greek sauce, whose name means "egg and lemon." Serve the chicken with a simple bean or lentil dish, such as Yellow Split Pea Purée (page 138), or with couscous or brown rice.

1 Season the chicken with salt and pepper. Heat 2 tablespoons of the olive oil in a sauté pan over medium-high heat and brown the chicken on all sides, 5 to 10 minutes. Remove the chicken to a plate and pour off any fat from the pan.

2 Add the remaining tablespoon olive oil to the pan, then add the onion and garlic, and cook until the onion begins to color, 5 to 7 minutes. Add the tomato paste and mix well, and then add the juice of 1 of the lemons.

3 Return the chicken to the pan, add the brandy, and sprinkle with the cinnamon and salt and pepper. Add enough water to come halfway up the side of the chicken, then cover with a lid, and simmer over low heat for 25 minutes.

4 Add the artichokes to the pan and top up the water if necessary: the artichokes should be almost submerged. Cover and simmer gently until the chicken and artichokes are quite tender, 25 to 30 minutes.

5 Just before serving, make the avgolemono sauce: whisk together the eggs and juice of the remaining 2 lemons until the mixture is pale and light. Gradually whisk in a ladleful of the hot chicken cooking liquid, stirring constantly. Pour the mixture over and around the chicken and stir well. Remove the pan from the heat and continue stirring for about 3 minutes, or until the sauce thickens. Do not let the sauce boil or the eggs will curdle. Serve hot, sprinkled with the pine nuts.

PER SERVING GLYCEMIC LOAD 0; PROTEIN 70 G; CARBOHYDRATES 24 G; FAT 23 G (INCLUDES 5 G SATURATED FAT); FIBER 9 G

Chicken Kebabs with Fresh Herbs

SERVES 4

1½ pounds boneless, skinless chicken breast halves, cut into 1-inch chunks

4 tablespoons olive oil

4 garlic cloves, crushed

1 teaspoon dried mint

1 teaspoon dried oregano

Salt and pepper

2 tablespoons fresh lemon juice

1 bunch fresh mint

1 eggplant, cut into 1-inch chunks

1 red onion, cut into wedges

1 red or yellow bell pepper, cut into 1-inch chunks

1 lemon, cut into 8 wedges

This aromatic grilled chicken with vegetables and herbs pairs wonderfully with Greek Salad (page 82).

1 Mix the chicken, 2 tablespoons of the olive oil, the garlic, dried mint and oregano, a pinch of salt, and 1 teaspoon pepper in a bowl and let marinate for 30 minutes.

2 Preheat the broiler until very hot or heat the grill to high.

3 Whisk the remaining 2 tablespoons olive oil with the lemon juice.

4 Thread the chicken, mint leaves, eggplant, onion, and bell pepper onto 8 metal skewers. Add a lemon wedge to each end. Sprinkle with salt and pepper and brush with the oil and lemon mixture. Cook, turning and basting with the oil and lemon mixture, until the chicken is just cooked through, about 9 minutes. Serve at once.

PER SERVING GLYCEMIC LOAD 2; PROTEIN 41 G; CARBOHYDRATES 15 G; FAT 16 G (INCLUDES 2 G SATURATED FAT); FIBER 5 G

MAKE AHEAD The chicken can be marinated in the refrigerator up to 8 hours in advance. The kebabs can be assembled up to 2 hours before cooking and stored in the refrigerator.

Chicken with Chile and Lemon Thyme

SERVES 4

1 tablespoon clarified butter

4 boneless, skinless chicken breast halves (about 5 ounces each)

2 tablespoons sweet Thai chile sauce

1 tablespoon finely chopped fresh lemon thyme

Salt

If you can't obtain lemon thyme, try this with basil instead. Serve with stir-fried vegetables such as snow peas, red or yellow bell peppers, and bean sprouts.

1 Preheat the oven to 250°F or the lowest setting.

2 Heat the butter in a heavy, nonstick skillet over medium heat. Add the chicken breasts and brown on both sides, 3 to 5 minutes per side. Transfer them to a baking dish.

3 Mix the chile sauce with the thyme. Brush over the chicken breasts and sprinkle with a little salt. Place the chicken in the oven and roast until cooked through, about 30 minutes. Serve hot.

PER SERVING GLYCEMIC LOAD 0; PROTEIN 33 G; CARBOHYDRATES 2 G; FAT 5 G (INCLUDES 2 G SATURATED FAT); FIBER 0 G

Parmesan-Coated Chicken

SERVES 4

1 tablespoon clarified butter

4 boneless, skinless chicken breast halves (about 5 ounces each)

½ cup finely grated Parmesan cheese

Freshly ground black pepper

Say "cheese" and smile, for this easy dish tastes fantastic.

1 Preheat the oven to 325°F.

2 Put a little clarified butter in a heavy skillet, preferably nonstick, over medium-high heat. When the butter is very hot, add the chicken breasts and brown them quickly on both sides, about 5 minutes per side. Remove from the heat and let cool slightly.

3 Spread the Parmesan on a plate and season with pepper. Turn the chicken breasts in the Parmesan to coat all over and then arrange them in a baking dish. Place in the oven and bake until cooked through, about 10 minutes. When the chicken is pierced with a knife, the juices should run clear. Serve hot.

PER SERVING GLYCEMIC LOAD 0; PROTEIN 37 G; CARBOHYDRATES 0 G; FAT 10 G (INCLUDES 5 G SATURATED FAT); FIBER 0 G

Chicken with Shallots and Cinnamon

SERVES 6

2 tablespoons clarified butter

6 skinless chicken legs,
or 6 thighs and 6 drumsticks

14 ounces small shallots or pearl
onions, peeled

1¼ cups chicken broth

1 teaspoon ground cinnamon

1 teaspoon fructose powder

½ teaspoon finely chopped
fresh rosemary

Salt and pepper

⅓ cup pine nuts, lightly toasted

1 tablespoon olive oil

Serve with steamed vegetables such as green beans, zucchini, leeks, or carrots and spoon the aromatic cooking liquid over the chicken and vegetables.

1 If using chicken legs, divide each leg into thighs and drumsticks, cutting at the joint.

2 Melt 1 tablespoon of the butter in a large skillet over medium-high heat. Add the chicken and brown on all sides, 8 to 10 minutes. Remove the chicken from the pan and set aside.

3 Wipe out the pan with a paper towel. Melt the remaining tablespoon butter in the pan. Add the shallots and cook over low heat until softened and golden, but not brown, 5 to 7 minutes.

4 Return the chicken pieces to the pan. Pour in the broth, add the cinnamon, fructose, and rosemary, and season with salt and pepper. Bring to a boil over high heat, then reduce the heat, and simmer until the chicken meat is falling off the bone, about 40 minutes.

5 Serve hot, sprinkling each serving with pine nuts and a few drops of olive oil.

PER SERVING GLYCEMIC LOAD 0; PROTEIN 30 G; CARBOHYDRATES 13 G; FAT 16 G (INCLUDES 5 G SATURATED FAT); FIBER 1 G

MAKE AHEAD Cook the chicken up to 2 days in advance and store in the refrigerator; reheat thoroughly. Alternatively, double the quantities and freeze half.

◄ Chicken with Tomatoes and Ouzo

SERVES 4

3 tablespoons olive oil

1 chicken (about 3½ pounds),
cut into 8 pieces

Salt and pepper

6 garlic cloves, chopped

1½ teaspoons fennel seeds,
crushed, or 1 teaspoon ground
star anise

2 15-ounce cans plum tomatoes,
drained

½ cup chicken broth

⅓ cup ouzo or additional
chicken broth

1 tablespoon dried oregano

12 black olives, pitted

4 ounces feta cheese,
crumbled (1 cup)

*If you haven't got a bottle of ouzo left over from a Greek holiday,
use another anise-flavored liqueur such as Pernod or Ricard.*

1 Heat the oil in a large sauté pan over medium-high heat. Add the
chicken, season with salt and pepper, and brown thoroughly on all sides,
8 to 10 minutes. Remove to a plate.

2 Pour off all but 2 tablespoons of fat from the pan. Add the garlic and
fennel seeds and stir for 30 seconds. Add the tomatoes, broth, ouzo, and
oregano. Bring to a boil, crushing the tomatoes with the back of a spoon.
Return the chicken to the pan and bring to a boil, lower the heat and
simmer for 15 minutes. Turn over the chicken pieces and simmer for 5
minutes. Remove the chicken from the sauce and keep warm.

3 Add the olives to the sauce and boil over high heat, stirring frequently,
until it thickens, 6 to 8 minutes. Season with salt and pepper to taste.
Serve the chicken on warmed plates, spoon the sauce over, sprinkle the
feta cheese on top, and serve immediately.

PER SERVING GLYCEMIC LOAD 1; PROTEIN 56 G; CARBOHYDRATES 27 G; FAT 39 G
(INCLUDES 10 G SATURATED FAT); FIBER 4 G

MAKE AHEAD This recipe can be made a day in advance and
refrigerated. Add the feta cheese just before serving.

Spicy Lemon Chicken

SERVES 6

6 skinless chicken legs or
6 thighs and 6 drumsticks

Grated zest and juice of 2 lemons

4 garlic cloves, finely chopped

1 large onion, finely chopped

1 teaspoon sambal oelek
(Indonesian chile sauce)

2 tablespoons olive oil

Salt and pepper

¼ cup chopped fresh parsley

*Serve with cucumber or carrot salad or roasted vegetables as well as
a dish of lentils or beans.*

1 If using chicken legs, divide each leg into thighs and drumsticks,
cutting at the joint.

2 Mix together the lemon zest and juice, garlic, onion, sambal oelek,
olive oil, and some salt and pepper. Place the chicken and lemon
mixture in a resealable plastic bag and seal well. Leave the chicken to
marinate in the refrigerator overnight.

3 Preheat the oven to 250°F or the lowest setting.

4 Take the chicken out of the marinade and place in a roasting pan. Roast
until cooked through, about 1 hour. When the chicken is pierced with a
knife, the juices should run clear. Serve hot, sprinkled with the parsley

PER SERVING GLYCEMIC LOAD 0; PROTEIN 27 G; CARBOHYDRATES 5 G; FAT 9.5 G
(INCLUDES 2 G SATURATED FAT); FIBER 0.5 G

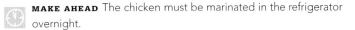

MAKE AHEAD The chicken must be marinated in the refrigerator
overnight.

Slow-Roasted Turkey Breast with Herbed Olive Oil

SERVES 4

⅓ cup olive oil

¼ cup chopped fresh herbs, such as basil, thyme, or parsley

1 boneless turkey breast half (about 1½ pounds)

Salt and pepper

Serve this aromatic roast with Roasted Mixed Vegetables (page 126) or a tomato salad.

1 Preheat the oven to 250°F or the lowest setting.

2 Put the oil and herbs in a blender (or use a hand-held blender) and blend until smooth, green, and thick.

3 Place the turkey in a roasting pan. Using a spoon or brush, coat the breast generously with the herbed oil and season with a little salt and pepper. If you have a roasting thermometer, insert it into the thickest part of the meat and set the thermometer to a desired temperature of 150°F.

4 Place the turkey in the oven. The roasting time will vary depending on the thickness of the breast, but it will be about 1½ hours. When the turkey is done, its juices will run clear when it is pierced with a knife. If the turkey breast is cooked before you are ready to serve it, open the oven door, but leave the turkey in the oven to keep warm.

4 Slice against the grain and serve hot.

PER SERVING GLYCEMIC LOAD 0; PROTEIN 42 G; CARBOHYDRATES 0 G; FAT 25 G (INCLUDES 4 G SATURATED FAT); FIBER 0 G

 MAKE AHEAD The herbed oil can be made up to 3 days in advance; store in a jar in the refrigerator and stir well before using.

Garlic and Rosemary-Scented Turkey

SERVES 4

2 whole bulbs garlic

2 tablespoons butter, melted

2 tablespoons olive oil

1 tablespoon finely
chopped fresh rosemary

1 tablespoon Dijon mustard

½ teaspoon salt

½ teaspoon freshly ground black
pepper

1 boneless turkey breast half
(about 1½ pounds)

1 tablespoon clarified butter

*I just love the combination of rosemary and mustard, which is great
with lamb as well as turkey. You can easily make variations on this
recipe by using tarragon, thyme, oregano, or basil instead of rosemary.*

1 Preheat the oven to 350°F.

2 To make the garlic paste, cut the top ½ inch or so off the garlic
bulbs—just enough to reveal the cloves. Place the garlic, cut side up, in
a small ovenproof skillet. Drizzle the melted butter over the garlic and
cover the pan with aluminum foil. Roast until the garlic is completely soft
but not browned, about 1 hour 20 minutes. Take the pan out of the
oven, remove the foil, and leave the garlic to cool for about 45 minutes.

3 Reduce the oven temperature to 250°F or the lowest setting.

4 Squeeze the garlic cloves out of the bulbs one by one and put them in
a blender or food processor. Add the olive oil, rosemary, mustard, salt,
and pepper and process to a smooth paste. Set aside.

5 Melt the clarified butter in a large, ovenproof skillet over medium-
high heat. Add the turkey and brown on all sides, 8 to 10 minutes.
Spread a generous layer of garlic paste over the surface of the turkey.
If you have a roasting thermometer, insert it into the thickest part of the
meat and set the thermometer to a desired temperature of 150°F. Place
in the oven and roast until cooked through, about 1½ hours, depending
on the thickness of the breast. When the turkey is done, its juices will run
clear when it is pierced with a knife.

6 Slice against the grain and serve hot.

PER SERVING GLYCEMIC LOAD 0; PROTEIN 42 G; CARBOHYDRATES 1 G; FAT 16 G
(INCLUDES 7 G SATURATED FAT); FIBER 0 G

MAKE AHEAD The garlic paste may be made up to 2 days in
advance and stored in a jar in the refrigerator. Make double or
treble quantities for use in other recipes: On chicken breasts, leg of
lamb or lamb cutlets.

Souvlaki with Red Pepper Sauce ▶

SERVES 4

¼ cup olive oil

Juice of 1 lemon

2 teaspoons fresh thyme or 1
teaspoon dried

2 garlic cloves, crushed

Freshly ground black pepper

1¾ pounds lean boneless leg of
lamb, trimmed and
cut into 1-inch pieces

8 to 12 bay leaves, preferably fresh

1 lemon, cut into wedges, to serve

RED PEPPER SAUCE

6 red bell peppers, halved and
seeded

2 tablespoons olive oil

6 garlic cloves, finely chopped

1 small red chile pepper, seeded and
finely chopped (optional)

2 tablespoons red wine vinegar

1 teaspoon cold-pressed flaxseed oil

2 teaspoons dried oregano or mint

Salt and pepper

*This delicious dish tastes best prepared on a grill, though a grill pan
and 250°F oven can be used when the weather does not cooperate.*

1 To marinate the lamb, mix the olive oil, lemon juice, thyme, garlic, and
a little pepper in a bowl. Add the lamb and mix well to coat. Refrigerate
for at least 2 hours, or overnight.

2 Meanwhile, preheat the oven to 425°F to make the sauce.

3 Put the peppers in a small roasting pan and rub with 1 tablespoon of
the olive oil. Roast until the peppers begin to brown, 20 to 30 minutes.
Put the peppers into a plastic bag, seal, and let sit for 10 minutes to
loosen the skins.

4 Peel the peppers and put them into a blender or food processor with
the remaining tablespoon olive oil, garlic, chile pepper, vinegar, flaxseed
oil, and oregano. Blend until completely smooth. Season with salt and
pepper.

5 Preheat half of the grill to high and half to low.

6 Thread the meat onto 4 skewers, with the bay leaves. Grill the kebabs
over high heat until browned on all sides, 5 to 7 minutes. Brush the
kebabs with any remaining marinade and transfer to the cooler part of
the grill. Cover and finish cooking until just pink inside, about 10 minutes.
Serve with lemon wedges and the red pepper sauce.

PER SERVING GLYCEMIC LOAD 0; PROTEIN 37 G; CARBOHYDRATES 11 G; FAT 35 G
(INCLUDES 8 G SATURATED FAT); FIBER 3 G

Lamb Meatballs

SERVES 4

9 ounces lean ground lamb

9 ounces lean ground beef

1 onion, finely chopped

1 tomato, finely chopped

2 garlic cloves, finely chopped

½ red bell pepper, finely chopped

½ small red chile pepper, seeded
and finely chopped

1 teaspoon chopped fresh
rosemary

2 large eggs

Salt and pepper

1 tablespoon clarified butter

*Serve with Tzatziki (page 87) and a bean or lentil dish such
as Yellow Split Pea Purée (page 138).*

1 Preheat the oven to 250°F or the lowest setting.

2 Mix together the lamb, beef, onion, tomato, garlic, bell and chile
peppers, rosemary, and eggs in a bowl. Season with salt and pepper.
Shape the mixture into 1½-inch meatballs.

3 Melt the butter in a large ovenproof skillet over medium-high heat.
Add the meatballs, in batches if necessary, and brown them on all sides,
5 to 7 minutes. Finish cooking in the oven until cooked through, 15 to 20
minutes. (Do not overcook or they will become dry.) Serve hot.

PER SERVING GLYCEMIC LOAD 0; PROTEIN 29 G; CARBOHYDRATES 7 G; FAT 18 G
(INCLUDES 8 G SATURATED FAT); FIBER 1.5 G

Lamb with Apricots and Almonds

SERVES 4

2 tablespoons clarified butter

1½ pounds lean lamb, cut into 1½-inch cubes

1 onion, coarsely chopped

2 garlic cloves, finely chopped

1 tablespoon ground coriander

2 teaspoons ground cumin

3 cups chicken or vegetable broth

A little grated fresh ginger

2 carrots, cut into large pieces

6 ounces green beans, fresh or frozen

3 ounces dried apricots, chopped

A handful of almonds, coarsely chopped

Salt and pepper

This wonderful dish is a fusion of Mediterranean and Indian flavors.

1 Melt 1 tablespoon of the butter in a large skillet over medium-high heat. Add the lamb and brown on all sides, 5 to 7 minutes. Remove the meat from the pan and set aside.

2 Melt the rest of the butter in the skillet, add the onion, garlic, coriander, and cumin, and let it color slightly, about 5 minutes. Return the meat to the pan, add the broth and ginger, and simmer over low heat until the meat is really tender, 40 minutes.

3 Add the carrots and cook for 10 minutes. Add the beans and apricots and cook until the carrots and beans are tender, 3 to 5 minutes. Add the almonds and season to taste with salt and pepper. Serve hot.

PER SERVING GLYCEMIC LOAD 5; PROTEIN 37 G; CARBOHYDRATES 26 G; FAT 27 G (INCLUDES 9 G SATURATED FAT); FIBER 6 G

MAKE AHEAD Refrigerate for up to 3 days or freeze for 2 months. Add the almonds just before serving.

Fricassée of Lamb

1½ pounds lean lamb, cut into
1½-inch cubes

Bouquet garni (celery, parsley
and thyme, wrapped in a piece
of leek and tied with string)

3 cups chicken broth or water

3 carrots

2 slices rutabaga, each 1 inch thick

1 small celery root

½ cup half-and-half

3 tablespoons cornstarch

Salt and pepper

2 tablespoons chopped
fresh parsley or dill

This hearty stew is perfect for dinner on a cold winter's evening.

1 Put the meat and bouquet garni in a large saucepan and add the broth. Bring to a boil, then immediately reduce the heat, and simmer gently, skimming the surface occasionally, until the meat is tender, 45 minutes to 1 hour.

2 Meanwhile bring a medium saucepan of lightly salted water to a boil. Peel the carrots, rutabaga, and celery root and cut into 1-inch dice. Cook in the boiling water until al dente (still with a bit of bite), 15 minutes for carrots and rutabaga and 10 for celery root. Drain and refresh the vegetables under cold water. Drain well.

3 When the meat is tender, remove the bouquet garni and transfer the meat to a warmed dish. Strain the broth into a clean saucepan. Add the half-and-half and bring to a boil. Dissolve the cornstarch in a little cold water and stir it into the boiling liquid. Cook, whisking, for 1 minute. Season with salt and pepper.

4 Return the meat and vegetables to the sauce and heat through for a few minutes. Stir in the parsley and serve hot.

PER SERVING GLYCEMIC LOAD 11; PROTEIN 33 G; CARBOHYDRATES 12 G; FAT 15 G (INCLUDES 7 G SATURATED FAT); FIBER 1.5 G

Roast Lamb with Herbs and Garlic

3 tablespoons olive oil

1 tablespoon finely chopped fresh
rosemary

1 tablespoon finely chopped
fresh thyme

2 tablespoons chopped
fresh parsley

Salt and pepper

1 boned leg of lamb, weighing
2 to 2½ pounds, tied

2 to 3 garlic cloves,
cut into slivers

This delicious, juicy roast is fragrant with Mediterranean herbs.

1 Preheat the oven to 250°F or the lowest setting.

2 Combine the olive oil, rosemary, thyme, and parsley in a blender until smooth. Season with salt and pepper.

3 Using a small sharp knife, make small pockets in the meat and insert the slivers of garlic. Heat a large roasting pan over medium heat and brown the meat all over, about 10 minutes. Brush the herbed oil over the meat. Transfer to the oven and roast until the meat registers 150°F on a meat thermometer for medium (pink) meat, about 2 hours. Let rest for 15 minutes before slicing.

PER SERVING GLYCEMIC LOAD 0; PROTEIN 24 G; CARBOHYDRATES 1 G; FAT 15 G (INCLUDES 4 G SATURATED FAT); FIBER 0 G

Pork Casserole with Chickpeas and Orange

1½ cups dried chickpeas

3 tablespoons clarified butter

1½ pounds pork shoulder, cut into 1½-inch cubes

2 onions, sliced

2 garlic cloves, finely chopped

½ small red chile pepper, seeded and finely chopped

1 15-ounce can chopped tomatoes

Grated zest of 1 orange

Salt and pepper

2 tablespoons olive oil

If you are in a hurry, use canned chickpeas for this spicy, orange-scented dish.

1 Soak the chickpeas in a generous amount of water overnight.

2 Drain the chickpeas and put them in a large saucepan. Add fresh water to a finger's width above the chickpeas. Put on the lid, bring to a boil over high heat, and cook for 10 minutes. Reduce the heat and simmer gently, skimming occasionally, until the chickpeas are soft, about 1 hour. Drain the chickpeas, retaining the cooking water.

3 Melt the butter in a heavy saucepan over medium-high heat and add the pork. Brown the meat on all sides, about 10 minutes. Transfer to a plate and set aside.

4 Put the onions in the saucepan and cook over medium heat until golden, about 10 minutes. Add the garlic and chile and cook for a few seconds. Add the tomatoes and orange zest and bring to a boil.

5 Add the chickpeas and meat to the tomato mixture. Add enough cooking water from the chickpeas to cover. Grind in a little pepper and mix well. Bring to a boil, then reduce the heat, and simmer, stirring occasionally, until the meat and chickpeas are tender, about 1 hour. Add more water if necessary as the meat and chickpeas cook to keep them moist.

6 Season to taste and serve in warmed soup plates; drizzle the olive oil on top before serving.

PER SERVING GLYCEMIC LOAD 8; PROTEIN 23 G; CARBOHYDRATES 38 G; FAT 17 G (INCLUDES 6 G SATURATED FAT); FIBER 9 G

 MAKE AHEAD This dish can be made a day in advance. Alternatively, it can be frozen for up to 2 months.

One-Pot Casserole with Cinnamon

SERVES 4

2 tablespoons clarified butter

1 pound lean ground beef

1 onion, finely chopped

4 ounces button mushrooms, sliced

1 15-ounce can chopped tomatoes

1 teaspoon dried thyme

½ teaspoon ground cinnamon

2 carrots, cut into chunks

1 small leek, white and light green parts, sliced

¾ cup red lentils, rinsed

Salt and pepper

2 teaspoons fructose powder (optional)

2 tablespoons olive oil

1 tablespoon chopped fresh parsley

A straightforward recipe for a hearty casserole.

1 Melt 1 tablespoon of the butter in a large skillet and add the beef and onion. Brown over medium-high heat, breaking up the meat with a wooden spoon. As soon as the meat has lost its redness, 5 to 7 minutes, transfer to a large saucepan.

2 Melt the remaining tablespoon butter in the skillet and add the mushrooms. Brown lightly, about 5 minutes, and add to the saucepan. Add the tomatoes, 1¼ cups water, thyme, and cinnamon to the saucepan. Bring to a simmer and cook for about 10 minutes. Add the carrots, leek, and lentils and cook until the lentils are soft, 15 to 20 minutes.

3 Season the casserole with salt and pepper, and fructose if you like. Serve hot, drizzled with olive oil and sprinkled with parsley.

PER SERVING GLYCEMIC LOAD 7; PROTEIN 36 G; CARBOHYDRATES 37 G; FAT 20 G (INCLUDES 7 G SATURATED FAT); FIBER 9 G

MAKE AHEAD This dish can be made up to 5 days in advance or frozen for 2 months.

Ragout of Beef with Onions

SERVES 4

3 tablespoons clarified butter

1½ pounds lean beef, cut into 2-inch cubes

1 cup canned chopped tomatoes

2 tablespoons tomato paste

2 onions, coarsely chopped

2 garlic cloves, finely chopped

½ teaspoon ground cinnamon

1 teaspoon dried thyme

Salt and pepper

2 tablespoons olive oil

3 tablespoons chopped fresh parsley

This is a traditional Greek dish called kokkinisto, *meaning red. The combination of onions, garlic, cinnamon, and tomatoes is very tasty.*

1 Melt 1½ tablespoons of the butter in a heavy saucepan over medium-high heat. Add the meat and brown on all sides, 8 to 10 minutes.

2 Add the tomatoes, tomato paste, and 1¾ cups water. Bring to a boil, lower the heat, and simmer for 15 minutes.

3 Meanwhile, melt the remaining 1½ tablespoons butter in a medium skillet. Add the onions and garlic and cook until golden, about 5 minutes. Add this to the meat, together with the cinnamon, thyme, and a little salt and pepper. Cover and simmer, adding more water if necessary, until the meat is completely tender, about 1½ hours.

4 Serve hot, drizzled with olive oil and sprinkled with parsley.

PER SERVING GLYCEMIC LOAD 0; PROTEIN 36 G; CARBOHYDRATES 13 G; FAT 26 G (INCLUDES 10 G SATURATED FAT); FIBER 2 G

MAKE AHEAD This dish can be made up to 5 days in advance or frozen for 2 months.

Stuffed Peppers

SERVES 4

4 medium or 8 small bell peppers

2 tablespoons olive oil

1 pound lean ground beef, lamb, or pork

1 onion, finely chopped

2 garlic cloves

½ small red chile pepper, seeded and finely chopped

1 tablespoon dried thyme

2 teaspoons Dijon mustard

1 teaspoon fructose powder

1 15-ounce can chopped tomatoes

3 tablespoons tomato paste

Salt and pepper

Chopped fresh parsley and oregano, to serve

You could use tomatoes or zucchini instead of the peppers; the cooking time will be slightly shorter.

1 Preheat the oven to 325°F.

2 Slice off the tops of the bell peppers and reserve. Scrape out the seeds.

3 Heat 1 tablespoon of the oil in a saucepan over medium heat. Add the meat, onion, garlic, and chile and stir over the heat until the meat looks crumbly and has lost its redness, 5 to 7 minutes. Add the thyme, mustard, fructose, tomatoes, tomato paste, and 1¾ cups water and simmer until the mixture has thickened slightly, about 15 minutes. Remove from the heat and season with salt and pepper.

4 Fill the peppers with the meat mixture; do not overfill. Place the filled peppers in a baking dish just large enough to hold them snugly. Cover with the reserved tops and brush with the remaining tablespoon olive oil.

5 Bake until the peppers are tender, 50 to 60 minutes. You may want to add a little boiling water to the baking dish during cooking if the vegetables look dry. Serve hot, sprinkled with parsley and oregano.

PER SERVING GLYCEMIC LOAD 0; PROTEIN 25 G; CARBOHYDRATES 20 G; FAT 15 G (INCLUDES 4 G SATURATED FAT); FIBER 5 G

MAKE AHEAD The meat filling can be made 2 days ahead and stored in the refrigerator. It could also be frozen for 2 months. This stuffing can also be used as a sauce for pasta.

Ragout of Venison with Mushrooms and Lentils

SERVES 4

2 tablespoons clarified butter

1 onion, finely chopped

4 ounces button mushrooms

4 ounces chanterelle mushrooms

1 pound loin of venison, cut into 1½-inch cubes

1 15-ounce can chopped tomatoes

2 cups beef broth or water

1 teaspoon dried thyme

1 to 2 teaspoons fructose powder

½ teaspoon ground cinnamon

2 carrots, cut into chunks

1 small leek, white and light green parts, sliced

¾ cup red lentils, rinsed

3 tablespoons sour cream (optional), plus extra to serve

Salt and pepper

1 tablespoon chopped fresh parsley (optional)

1 Melt 1 tablespoon of the butter in a skillet over medium heat, add the onion, and cook until soft and golden, 5 to 10 minutes. Transfer to a large saucepan. Melt the remaining 1 tablespoon butter in the skillet and cook the button and chanterelle mushrooms until just tender, 5 to 7 minutes. Add to the pan with the onion.

2 Add the venison, tomatoes, broth, thyme, 1 teaspoon fructose, and the cinnamon. Bring to a boil, then immediately reduce the heat, and simmer for 10 minutes. Add the carrots, leek, and lentils and cook until the lentils are soft, 15 to 20 minutes.

3 Stir in the sour cream and heat through. Season with salt and pepper and up to 1 teaspoon more fructose if necessary. Serve hot, sprinkled with parsley and a spoonful of cream if you like.

PER SERVING GLYCEMIC LOAD 7; PROTEIN 40 G; CARBOHYDRATES 39 G; FAT 10 G (INCLUDES 5 G SATURATED FAT); FIBER 9 G

Rabbit Casserole with Mavrodaphne

SERVES 4

1 rabbit (about 3½ pounds), cut
into 10 to 12 pieces

1 cup white wine vinegar

2 tablespoons clarified butter

12 to 14 pearl onions, peeled

½ cup Mavrodaphne,
Madeira, or port

3 carrots, sliced

2 bay leaves

½ teaspoon ground cloves

1 cinnamon stick

Salt and pepper

½ cup olive oil

2 tablespoons coarsely
chopped walnuts

Mavrodaphne is a sweet, fortified Greek wine made from the aromatic mavrodaphne grape. Look for it in wine shops, but if it isn't available, you can use Madeira or port as an alternative.

1 Put the rabbit meat in a large bowl. Mix the vinegar with 1 cup water and pour over the rabbit. Leave to marinate for 2 hours.

2 Melt 1 tablespoon of the butter in a wide, heavy saucepan over medium heat. Add the onions and cook until soft and golden, about 10 minutes. Remove from the pan and set aside.

3 Remove the rabbit from the marinade and pat dry with paper towels. Melt the remaining tablespoon butter in the saucepan over medium-high heat, add the rabbit, and brown lightly all over, about 10 minutes.

4 Return the onions to the saucepan and pour in the Mavrodaphne. Add the carrots, bay leaves, cloves, cinnamon, and a little pepper and then add the olive oil and ½ cup water. Cover the pan and cook over medium heat until the meat is tender and falling off the bone, about 50 minutes.

5 Season to taste with salt and discard the bay leaves. Serve hot, sprinkled with the chopped walnuts.

PER SERVING GLYCEMIC LOAD 0; PROTEIN 64 G; CARBOHYDRATES 12 G; FAT 49 G (INCLUDES 12 G SATURATED FAT); FIBER 2 G

Roasted Mixed Vegetables

SERVES 6

2 small sweet potatoes

1 celery root

2 zucchini

1 small eggplant

1 red bell pepper

1 green bell pepper

2 to 3 carrots

2 to 3 onions

1 large leek, white and light green parts

1 pound ripe tomatoes

4 garlic cloves

¼ cup fresh oregano or 2 tablespoons dried

1 rosemary sprig

Small bunch fresh mint or 2 teaspoons dried, plus extra for sprinkling

Small bunch fresh parsley, plus extra for sprinkling

½ cup olive oil

Salt and pepper

In Greece, this traditional dish is known as briam. Serve it on its own or as an accompaniment to chicken or roast meat. Don't worry if you don't have all the vegetables; just increase the quantities of the ones you have to hand or substitute others. Okra and peas are often used in Greece, for example. Preparing the vegetables for this recipe takes a little time but the end result is worth the effort.

1 Preheat the oven to 350°F.

2 Cut into 1½- to 2-inch chunks the sweet potatoes, celery root, zucchini, eggplant, red and green peppers, and carrots. Cut the onions into wedges and the leek into thick rings. Peel and coarsely chop the tomatoes. Chop the garlic. Finely chop the oregano, rosemary, mint, and parsley.

3 Combine all of the vegetables and herbs in a roasting pan. Add the olive oil, season with salt and pepper, and mix well. Cover with foil and roast for 40 minutes.

4 Remove the foil and return the pan to the oven until the vegetables begin to color, about 15 minutes. Remove from the oven and serve warm.

PER SERVING GLYCEMIC LOAD 10; PROTEIN 4 G; CARBOHYDRATES 32 G; FAT 17 G (INCLUDES 2.5 G SATURATED FAT); FIBER 7 G

Vegetarian Moussaka

8 large eggplants, sliced

10 zucchini, sliced

10 bell peppers (red, orange, yellow and green), cut into rings

6 tablespoons olive oil

3 onions, finely chopped

Salt and pepper

Fructose powder

8 to 10 tomatoes, peeled and coarsely chopped

3 tablespoons freshly grated Parmesan cheese

15 slices Edam or other mild cheese

In Greece, this would be topped with a mild cows' milk cheese called Kaseri; Edam is a good substitute.

1 Preheat the oven to 425°F.

2 Put the eggplants, zucchini, and peppers in a roasting pan, drizzle with 3 tablespoons of the oil and roast until tender, about 40 minutes.

3 Meanwhile, heat the remaining 3 tablespoons oil in a saucepan, add the onions and salt, pepper, and fructose to taste and cook over medium heat until the onions begin to soften, about 5 minutes. Add the tomatoes and a few tablespoons water and simmer until you have a thick sauce, about 15 minutes.

4 Place a layer of roasted eggplants in a lightly oiled, large baking dish. Season with salt and pepper and add some tomato sauce and Parmesan. Add a layer of zucchini, then peppers, and sauce. Continue layering until the dish is full. Lay the Edam slices on top.

5 Bake the moussaka for 15 minutes. Serve hot.

PER SERVING GLYCEMIC LOAD 2; PROTEIN 16 G; CARBOHYDRATES 35 G; FAT 18 G (INCLUDES 8 G SATURATED FAT); FIBER 15 G

Garlic Spinach

1½ to 2 pounds fresh spinach, stemmed

3 tablespoons olive oil

6 scallions or 1 leek, white and green parts, thinly sliced

2 garlic cloves, thinly sliced

Salt and pepper

2 tablespoons chopped fresh dill (optional)

Juice of ½ lemon

A delicious side dish, this is especially good with lamb. The dill adds a Greek touch.

1 Cut the spinach into ribbons about ½ inch wide. Place in a large saucepan with a teaspoon or two of water. Cook over low heat, stirring occasionally, until the spinach wilts, about 3 minutes. Drain thoroughly, squeezing out the excess water.

2 Heat 2 tablespoons of the olive oil in the pan, add the scallions and garlic and cook until the scallions begin to soften, 2 to 3 minutes.

3 Add the spinach and stir over medium heat for 2 to 3 minutes. Season with salt and pepper, add the dill, lemon juice, and the remaining tablespoon olive oil, and serve at once.

PER SERVING GLYCEMIC LOAD 0; PROTEIN 5 G; CARBOHYDRATES 10 G; FAT 11 G (INCLUDES 1 G SATURATED FAT); FIBER 5 G

Baked Eggplants in Tomato Sauce

SERVES 8

6 tablespoons olive oil

4 large eggplants, halved lengthwise

6 onions, sliced into rings

6 garlic cloves

Salt and pepper

6 large ripe tomatoes, peeled and coarsely chopped

2 tablespoons tomato paste

2 teaspoons fructose powder

1 tablespoon dried mint

Large bunch of parsley, finely chopped

¼ cup freshly grated Parmesan cheese

4 ounces Gruyère or Cheddar cheese, shredded (1 cup)

These baked eggplants are very popular in Greece, but the recipe is actually from Turkey, where it is known as Imam bayildi, *which means "the priest fainted"—presumably with delight.*

1 Preheat the oven to 350°F.

2 Heat 2 tablespoons of the oil in a large skillet over medium-high heat. Add the eggplants and cook until lightly browned, 3 minutes on each side. Drain on paper towels.

3 Heat the remaining 4 tablespoons oil in a large saucepan and add the onions, garlic, and salt and pepper to taste. Cook over medium-low heat until the onions are golden, about 20 minutes.

4 Add the tomatoes, tomato paste, fructose, mint, and parsley. Simmer over low heat until the mixture thickens, about 5 minutes.

5 Place the eggplants in a roasting pan, skin side down, and divide the tomato mixture among the eggplants. Mix the Parmesan and Gruyère together and sprinkle over the eggplants. Bake in the oven for 20 minutes. Serve warm.

PER SERVING GLYCEMIC LOAD 0; PROTEIN 10 G; CARBOHYDRATES 27 G; FAT 17 G (INCLUDES 5 G SATURATED FAT); FIBER 1 G

Leek, Mushroom, and Tomato Gratin

SERVES 4

1 tablespoon olive oil

1 onion, sliced

2 garlic cloves, finely chopped

2 large leeks, thinly sliced

7 ounces mushrooms, quartered

1 15-ounce can chopped tomatoes

2 tablespoons tomato paste

½ teaspoon dried oregano

½ teaspoon dried thyme

Salt and pepper

½ teaspoon fructose powder

⅓ cup crumbled feta cheese

This dish is just as delicious made with zucchini or fennel instead of leeks.

1 Heat the oil in a large skillet over low heat. Add the onion, garlic, and leeks and cook gently until the vegetables soften and begin to turn golden, 6 to 8 minutes.

2 Add the mushrooms and cook for 2 to 3 minutes. Add the tomatoes with their juice, tomato paste, oregano, and thyme. Simmer for 4 to 5 minutes. Season to taste with salt, pepper, and the fructose.

3 Preheat the broiler.

4 Put the vegetable mixture into a shallow baking dish and sprinkle the cheese on top. Place under the broiler until the cheese begins to brown and bubble, 2 to 3 minutes. Serve hot.

PER SERVING GLYCEMIC LOAD 0; PROTEIN 6 G; CARBOHYDRATES 20 G; FAT 6 G (INCLUDES SATURATES 2.5 G); FIBER 3.5 G

◄ Zucchini Gratin

This rich, creamy dish looks striking made with a mixture of green zucchini and yellow summer squash.

SERVES 4

2 large zucchini, sliced
⅔ cup crumbled feta cheese
4 large eggs
1¼ cups reduced-fat crème fraîche or sour cream
2 garlic cloves, finely chopped
Handful of basil leaves, chopped
Salt and pepper

1 Preheat the oven to 350°F.

2 Bring a saucepan of lightly salted water to a boil. Add the zucchini and cook for 2 minutes. Drain, cool under cold running water, and drain well. Arrange the zucchini in a shallow ovenproof dish. Sprinkle the feta cheese over the zucchini.

3 Mix the eggs with the crème fraîche, garlic, basil, and salt and pepper to taste. Pour over the zucchini and bake for 15 minutes.

4 Reduce the oven temperature to 300°F and cook for 20 minutes. The finished dish should not look too brown on top. Serve hot.

PER SERVING GLYCEMIC LOAD 0; PROTEIN 13 G; CARBOHYDRATES 8 G; FAT 18 G (INCLUDES 10 G SATURATED FAT); FIBER 2 G

Baked Zucchini and Fennel Omelet

SERVES 4

4 tablespoons olive oil
About 1 pound zucchini, grated
1 large red onion, finely chopped
1 bulb fennel, halved and thinly sliced
6 large eggs
Salt and pepper

1 Preheat the oven to 350°F. Grease a round ovenproof dish with 1 tablespoon of the oil.

2 Heat the remaining 3 tablespoons oil in a large sauté pan and add the zucchini. Stir over medium heat until the liquid released by the zucchini has evaporated, 3 to 5 minutes. Add the onion and fennel, reduce the heat slightly, and cook until the onion begins to soften, 8 to 10 minutes. Transfer to a bowl to cool for a few minutes.

3 Beat the eggs together with a little salt and pepper and mix them with the vegetables in the bowl. Pour the mixture into the prepared dish and bake until the omelet has set and the surface is golden, about 50 minutes.

4 Remove from the oven and leave to cool for a few minutes. Cut into slices and serve.

PER SERVING GLYCEMIC LOAD 0; PROTEIN 12 G; CARBOHYDRATES 12 G; FAT 21 G (INCLUDES 4 G SATURATED FAT); FIBER 4 G

Cauliflower with Tomatoes and Feta ▶

SERVES 4

2 tablespoons clarified butter

1 large onion, sliced

2 garlic cloves, crushed

8 tomatoes, peeled and finely chopped

2 teaspoons dried oregano

Pinch of ground cinnamon

Salt and pepper

1 large head cauliflower, cut into florets

3 tablespoons olive oil

1 tablespoon fresh lemon juice

½ cup crumbled feta cheese

This is particularly good with lamb or other grilled or roasted meat. Or serve with a bean or lentil dish and a salad for a vegetarian feast.

1 Preheat the oven to 375°F.

2 Melt the butter in a large skillet over medium heat, add the onion and garlic, and cook for 3 to 4 minutes. Add the tomatoes, oregano, cinnamon, and a little salt and pepper. Stir well, then cover, and simmer for approximately 5 minutes.

3 Add the cauliflower florets to the tomato sauce, cover, and simmer for 10 to 15 minutes.

4 Transfer to a baking dish and drizzle with the olive oil and lemon juice. Top with the feta.

5 Bake until the cauliflower is tender and the cheese has melted, about 40 minutes. Serve hot.

PER SERVING GLYCEMIC LOAD 0; PROTEIN 10 G; CARBOHYDRATES 28 G; FAT 21 G (INCLUDES 8 G SATURATED FAT); FIBER 9.5 G

Broccoli Mustard Gratin

SERVES 6

2 heads broccoli, cut into florets

¾ cup half-and-half

¾ cup low-fat milk

1 tablespoon cornstarch

1 tablespoon Dijon mustard

2 ounces Gruyère or Cheddar cheese, shredded (½ cup)

Scant ½ cup freshly grated Parmesan cheese

Salt and pepper

Serve with a mixed salad or Tomato Salad with Beans and Basil (page 77) for a complete meal.

1 Preheat the oven to 425°F.

2 Cook the broccoli in lightly salted boiling water for 2 minutes; it should still be slightly crisp. Drain in a colander, rinse under cold water, and drain thoroughly.

3 Put the half-and-half and milk in a saucepan and bring to a boil over medium heat. Dissolve the cornstarch in a little water and whisk it into the hot mixture. Boil rapidly to thicken, about 2 minutes. Take the sauce off the heat and add the mustard and ¼ cup of the Gruyère and ¼ cup of the Parmesan. Season with salt and pepper and mix well.

4 Transfer the broccoli to a baking dish. Pour the sauce over the broccoli and sprinkle with the remaining ¼ cup each Gruyère and Parmesan. Bake until the top is golden, about 10 minutes.

PER SERVING GLYCEMIC LOAD 0; PROTEIN 12 G; CARBOHYDRATES 17 G; FAT 10 G (INCLUDES 6 G SATURATED FAT); FIBER 5 G

Baked Fennel with Peppers and Roasted Tomatoes

SERVES 4

4 plum tomatoes, halved

Salt and pepper

4 fennel bulbs,
each cut into 12 wedges

Scant ½ cup olive oil

2 garlic cloves, thinly sliced

1 red bell pepper,
thinly sliced

1 yellow bell pepper,
thinly sliced

½ teaspoon dried oregano

½ teaspoon dried thyme

Roasting tomatoes intensifies their flavor and gives them a firmer texture. I recommend that you roast more than the four needed for this recipe; extras are good in salads or added to chicken or meat dishes.

1 Preheat the oven to 250°F or the lowest setting.

2 Put the tomato halves, cut side up, on a baking sheet covered with parchment paper. Sprinkle the tomatoes with salt and place in the oven for 3 to 6 hours, depending on how moist you like them. The longer you leave them the more intense the flavor and the drier they will be— almost like sun-dried tomatoes.

3 Increase the oven temperature to 325°F. Put the fennel bulbs in a roasting pan, drizzle with ¼ cup of the oil, and season with salt and pepper. Cook, turning carefully once or twice, for 45 minutes.

4 Put the remaining ¼ cup oil in a saucepan over low heat. Add the garlic and cook for 2 minutes. Add the red and yellow peppers, oregano, and thyme, increase the heat, and sauté until the peppers are just tender, about 3 minutes. Add the tomatoes and fennel, stir gently, and simmer for 2 to 3 minutes. Season to taste with salt and pepper. Serve hot.

PER SERVING GLYCEMIC LOAD 0; PROTEIN 4 G; CARBOHYDRATES 23 G; FAT 24 G (INCLUDES 3 G SATURATED FAT); FIBER 9 G

 MAKE AHEAD You can prepare the roasted tomatoes in advance. They will keep for a week in the refrigerator.

Chickpea Fritters

SERVES 6

1½ cups dried chickpeas

8 tablespoons olive oil, or more, if needed

2 large onions, chopped

2 garlic cloves, crushed

1 teaspoon ground cumin

1 teaspoon dried thyme

3 tablespoons chopped fresh parsley

1 large egg, beaten

6 tablespoons chickpea flour, plus extra for coating

Salt and pepper

Serve with Greek Salad (page 82) as a main course or serve as a side dish or first course.

1 Soak the chickpeas in a generous amount of water overnight.

2 Rinse the chickpeas thoroughly. Place in a large saucepan with plenty of fresh water, bring to a boil, and cook for 10 minutes. Reduce the heat and simmer, skimming occasionally, until the chickpeas are very soft, about 1 hour. Drain, reserving about ½ cup of the cooking liquid.

3 Put the chickpeas in a food processor and blend to a paste, adding some of the cooking liquid to achieve a smooth consistency. Transfer the chickpea purée to a large bowl.

4 Heat 3 tablespoons of the oil in a large nonstick skillet over medium heat. Add the onions and cook until golden, about 5 minutes. Add the garlic and cumin and stir until fragrant, 1 to 2 minutes. Add the thyme and parsley, mix well, and remove from the heat.

5 Add the egg, chickpea flour, and onion mixture to the chickpea purée and mix thoroughly. Season with salt and pepper. Rinse your hands in cold water to prevent the mixture from sticking, then take walnut-sized balls of the chickpea mixture, and shape into flat patties. Coat in a little more chickpea flour. Place on a tray lined with parchment paper and refrigerate for at least 1 hour.

6 Heat the remaining 5 tablespoons oil in a large nonstick skillet over medium-high heat. Add the chickpea fritters in batches and cook until golden brown, 1 to 2 minutes per side. Remove with a slotted spoon and drain on paper towels. Keep warm while you cook the remaining fritters, adding more oil if necessary. Serve hot or at room temperature.

PER SERVING GLYCEMIC LOAD 5; PROTEIN 12 G; CARBOHYDRATES 38 G; FAT 22 G (INCLUDES 3 G SATURATED FAT); FIBER 9 G

 MAKE AHEAD The cooked fritters can be refrigerated for 3 to 4 days. The uncooked mixture can be frozen for up to 2 months.

Yellow Split Pea Purée

SERVES 6

1¼ cups chana dal or
yellow split peas

3 shallots, or 1 onion, quartered

1 garlic clove, peeled

5 tablespoons extra-virgin olive oil

1 teaspoon cold-pressed
flaxseed oil (optional)

2 tablespoons fresh lemon juice

Salt and ground white pepper

1 large bunch of scallions, white
and light green parts,
finely chopped

1 heaped tablespoon fresh thyme
or 1 teaspoon dried

chopped fresh parsley or oregano,
to serve

This is one of my childhood favorites. In Greece it is known as fava and it is served as an accompaniment to fish, meat, or vegetable dishes. The best yellow peas come from the volcanic island of Santorini.

1 Soak the split peas in a generous amount of water overnight.

2 Drain the peas and rinse well. Put the peas in a large saucepan (not cast-iron), together with the shallots and garlic. Add plenty of fresh water and bring to a boil. Reduce the heat and simmer gently, stirring and skimming occasionally, until the peas are very soft, 45 to 60 minutes.

3 Drain and reserve the cooking liquid. Remove the shallots and transfer the peas to a food processor. Add the olive oil, flaxseed oil, and lemon juice and blend until smooth and pale; add a little of the reserved cooking liquid if the purée seems too thick. Season to taste with salt and pepper. Add the scallions and thyme and stir well.

4 Spoon into a serving bowl and sprinkle with parsley. Serve hot or cold.

PER SERVING GLYCEMIC LOAD 3; PROTEIN 8 G; CARBOHYDRATES 27 G; FAT 14 G (INCLUDES 2 G SATURATED FAT); FIBER 2 G

 MAKE AHEAD This can be stored in the refrigerator for 4 to 5 days. It can also be frozen for up to 2 months.

White Beans with Tomatoes

SERVES 4 TO 6

1½ cups dried lima beans or other
large white beans

Scant ½ cup olive oil

2 large onions, chopped

2 carrots, diced

2 celery stalks, diced

3 garlic cloves, thinly sliced

1 teaspoon dried thyme

1 teaspoon dried oregano

1 15-ounce can
chopped tomatoes

2 tablespoons tomato paste

½ tablespoon fructose powder

Salt and pepper

3 tablespoons chopped
fresh parsley

This is a classic Greek dish known as gigantes plaki. *It can be served hot, warm, or cold.*

1 Soak the beans in a generous amount of water overnight.

2 Rinse the beans under cold water and place in a large saucepan. Add fresh water to cover and bring to a boil. Lower the heat and simmer until the beans are nearly soft, about 1 hour. Drain in a colander.

3 Preheat the oven to 350°F.

4 Heat the oil in a large saucepan over low heat, add the onions, and fry until light golden, about 10 minutes. Add the carrots, celery, garlic, thyme, and oregano and stir until fragrant, about 2 minutes.

5 Add the tomatoes and cook for 10 minutes. Add the tomato paste, 1¼ cups hot water, and the beans and mix well. Add the fructose, salt, and pepper to taste and mix well.

6 Pour the mixture into a baking dish and bake until the beans are tender, about 30 minutes. Test the beans occasionally and add more water if they seem dry.

7 Add the parsley and leave in the hot oven for 5 minutes before serving.

PER SERVING GLYCEMIC LOAD 14; PROTEIN 16 G; CARBOHYDRATES 56 G; FAT 25 G (INCLUDES 3.5 G SATURATED FAT); FIBER 16 G

 MAKE AHEAD This dish can be refrigerated for up to 5 days. It can also be frozen for 2 months.

Black Beans with Herbs

SERVES 2

1 15-ounce can black beans

2 tablespoons olive oil

2 shallots, finely chopped

2 tablespoons chopped
fresh parsley

1 teaspoon chopped fresh thyme

1 teaspoon chopped fresh oregano

Salt and pepper

*Did you know that black beans contain more antioxidants than
any other beans? Here is a simple yet delicious way to enjoy them.*

1 Drain the beans and rinse under cold running water. Place in a
saucepan, add water to cover, and heat through over low heat.

2 Meanwhile, heat 1 tablespoon of the oil in a medium skillet over
medium heat. Add the shallots and cook until translucent, 5 minutes. Add
the parsley, thyme, and oregano, then drain the beans thoroughly, and
add them to the skillet. Mix well and season to taste with salt and pepper.
Drizzle the remaining tablespoon olive oil over the top. Serve hot.

PER SERVING GLYCEMIC LOAD 6; PROTEIN 19 G; CARBOHYDRATES 52 G; FAT 15 G
(INCLUDES 2 G SATURATED FAT); FIBER 19 G

Puy Lentils with Red Wine

SERVES 2

1 cup Puy lentils or other green
lentils

Scant ½ cup red wine

2 shallots, finely chopped

2 tablespoons olive oil

2 tablespoons finely chopped
herbs or herb oil (page 68)

1 tablespoon balsamic vinegar

Salt and pepper

A little fructose powder

*Dark green Puy lentils are one of the tastiest varieties of lentil
and are a favorite of top chefs.*

1 Put the lentils in a saucepan with the wine and 1¼ cups water. Bring to
a boil, then reduce the heat, and simmer until tender—this will take
about 30 minutes. The cooking water should have been absorbed
completely; add more water during cooking if necessary.

2 Once the lentils are cooked, add the shallots, olive oil, herbs, and
vinegar and cook gently for 5 minutes. Season to taste with salt, pepper,
and fructose.

PER SERVING GLYCEMIC LOAD 12; PROTEIN 20 G; CARBOHYDRATES 57 G; FAT 15 G
(INCLUDES 2 G SATURATED FAT); FIBER 14 G

MAKE AHEAD This dish is best when fresh but leftovers can be
stored in the refrigerator for 3 to 4 days.

Mung Bean and Tomato Salad ▶

SERVES 4

SALAD

1 cup mung beans

Bunch of arugula (about 5 ounces)

1 large onion, finely chopped

2 large ripe tomatoes, chopped

4 sun-dried tomatoes,
cut into strips

2 tablespoons chopped
fresh parsley

2 tablespoons chopped walnuts

DRESSING

Scant ½ cup olive oil

1 tablespoon cold-pressed
flaxseed oil (optional)

1 tablespoon chopped
fresh cilantro

1 tablespoon chopped fresh thyme
or ½ tablespoon dried

1 tablespoon fresh lemon juice

½ teaspoon fructose powder

1 teaspoon Dijon mustard

Salt and pepper

Mung beans are tiny green beans that look very much like green lentils. They have a delicate nutty flavor and are packed with heart-healthy soluble fiber.

1 Put the mung beans in a saucepan with about 2 cups water. Boil until tender, about 40 minutes. Do not overcook or they will split. Drain thoroughly.

2 Soak the arugula in ice-cold water for 10 minutes then drain well, preferably in a salad spinner, and chop coarsely.

3 Combine the beans, onion, ripe and sun-dried tomatoes, arugula, and parsley in a bowl and mix gently.

4 Combine the olive oil, flaxseed oil, cilantro, thyme, lemon juice, fructose, mustard, and salt and pepper to taste and blend with a blender. Pour the dressing over the salad and mix gently. Sprinkle the walnuts over the top. Serve warm or cold.

PER SERVING GLYCEMIC LOAD 9; PROTEIN 12 G; CARBOHYDRATES 35 G; FAT 27 G (INCLUDES 4 G SATURATED FAT); FIBER 12.5 G

Lentil and Bean Salad

SERVES 4

¾ cup yellow lentils

1 15-ounce can red
kidney beans

1 15-ounce can chickpeas

2 ripe tomatoes, diced

1 tablespoon canned chipotle
chile, finely chopped

1 onion, finely chopped

1 garlic clove, finely chopped

3 tablespoons chopped
fresh cilantro

2 tablespoons white wine vinegar

¼ cup olive oil

1 teaspoon fructose powder

Salt and pepper

This recipe features a trio of pulses and has a Mexican influence.

1 Rinse the lentils under cold water until the water running off is clear. Put in a saucepan, cover with water, and bring to a boil. Cook until almost soft but still retaining a little bite, 12 to 14 minutes. Drain and rinse under cold water.

2 Rinse the beans and chickpeas under cold running water. Drain well and place in a large bowl with the lentils. Add the tomatoes, chipotle chile, onion, garlic, cilantro, vinegar, oil, fructose, and salt and pepper to taste and mix well. Serve warm or cold.

PER SERVING GLYCEMIC LOAD 14; PROTEIN 24 G; CARBOHYDRATES 73 G; FAT 18 G (INCLUDES 2 G SATURATED FAT); FIBER 19 G

MAKE AHEAD This dish can be made a day ahead and stored in the refrigerator.

Quinoa with Leek and Tomato

SERVES 4

1½ cups quinoa

½ teaspoon salt

1 tablespoon clarified butter

2 cups thinly sliced leeks, white
and light green parts

¼ cup chicken or vegetable broth

3 tablespoons olive oil

2 yellow or red tomatoes,
seeded and diced

3 tablespoons chopped
fresh chives

3 tablespoons chopped fresh basil

1 tablespoon fresh lemon juice

Salt and pepper

1 Place the quinoa in a strainer and rinse under cold running water until the water running off is clear. Put the quinoa and salt in a saucepan with 2 cups water and bring to a boil. Reduce the heat and simmer until the quinoa is almost tender and most of the water has disappeared. This will take around 20 minutes. Drain off the remaining water and set aside.

2 Melt the butter in a saucepan over medium heat. Add the leeks and sauté until soft, about 5 minutes. Add the broth, bring to a boil, and cook for about 5 minutes.

3 Add the quinoa and olive oil, mix well, and heat through for about 5 minutes. Finally, add the tomatoes, chives, basil, and lemon juice and stir gently for a few minutes, until heated through. Season to taste with salt and pepper. Serve hot or warm.

PER SERVING GLYCEMIC LOAD 15; PROTEIN 10 G; CARBOHYDRATES 54 G; FAT 17 G (INCLUDES 4 G SATURATED FAT); FIBER 5 G

Herbed Quinoa Pilaf

SERVES 8

4 cups quinoa

¾ teaspoon salt

3 tablespoons olive oil

1½ tablespoons fresh lemon juice

1½ cups pine nuts,
lightly toasted

1 red onion, finely chopped

1½ cups chopped fresh basil

Salt and pepper

1 Place the quinoa in a strainer and rinse under cold running water until the water running off is clear.

2 Put the quinoa and salt in a saucepan with 4 cups water and bring to a boil. Reduce the heat and simmer until the quinoa is almost tender and most of the water has disappeared. This will take around 20 minutes. Drain off the remaining water and transfer the quinoa to a large bowl.

3 Using a fork, stir in the olive oil and lemon juice and leave to cool to room temperature.

4 Stir in the pine nuts, red onion, and basil. Season to taste with salt and pepper. Serve at room temperature.

PER SERVING GLYCEMIC LOAD 20; PROTEIN 16 G; CARBOHYDRATES 64 G; FAT 27 G (INCLUDES 5 G SATURATED FAT); FIBER 8 G

Barley Risotto with Parmesan

SERVES 4

6 cups chicken broth

6 tablespoons clarified butter

1 onion, finely chopped

2 garlic cloves, finely chopped

2 cups pearl barley

4 ounces button mushrooms, sliced

Salt and pepper

½ cup freshly grated Parmesan cheese

1 tablespoon finely chopped fresh chives

1 tablespoon chopped fresh parsley

1 tablespoon chopped fresh basil

1 Bring the broth to a boil and keep warm.

2 Melt 2 tablespoons of the butter in a large saucepan over medium heat. Add the onion and garlic and sauté until the onion is soft but not brown, about 5 minutes. Add the barley and stir until the grains are lightly coated with butter.

3 Add ½ cup broth and let simmer, stirring frequently, until it is absorbed. Add the remaining broth ½ cup at a time, making sure the broth has been absorbed before adding more. Stir frequently so that the grains do not stick to the bottom of the pan. Cook until the barley is tender but still retains a little bite; the dish should look creamy. The cooking process takes around 45 minutes.

4 Meanwhile, melt 2 tablespoons of the butter in a skillet over medium-high heat. Add the mushrooms and sauté until tender, about 4 minutes.

5 Add the mushrooms, Parmesan, chives, parsley, basil, and the remaining 2 tablespoons butter to the barley. Mix well and season to taste with salt and pepper.

PER SERVING GLYCEMIC LOAD 22; PROTEIN 17 G; CARBOHYDRATES 85 G; FAT 24 G (INCLUDES 14 G SATURATED FAT); FIBER 16 G

Basmati Rice Salad with Nuts

SERVES 6

SALAD

2 cups brown basmati rice

1½ cups thinly sliced scallions, white and green parts

1½ cups finely chopped celery

¾ cup finely chopped fresh parsley

1 cup chopped walnuts

Salt and pepper

DRESSING

5 tablespoons olive oil

5 tablespoons fresh lemon juice

3 tablespoons soy sauce

2½ teaspoons ground cumin

1 Put the rice and 4 cups water in a saucepan and bring to a boil. Cover with a lid, reduce the heat, and simmer until the rice is tender, about 35 minutes. Drain off any excess water. Put the rice in a large bowl and stir with a fork to break up any clumps. Leave to cool.

2 Mix the scallions, celery, parsley, and walnuts into the rice.

3 Combine the oil, lemon juice, soy sauce, and cumin in a small bowl and mix well. Pour the dressing over the salad and mix everything well. Season to taste with salt and pepper.

PER SERVING GLYCEMIC LOAD 21; PROTEIN 10 G; CARBOHYDRATES 54 G; FAT 27 G (INCLUDES 3 G SATURATED FAT); FIBER 6 G

MAKE AHEAD This dish can be made 3 days ahead. It can also be made with leftover rice, though in this case the salad should be eaten immediately.

Peaches with Pomegranates and Rosemary ▶

This is a delightful and super-healthy dessert. Peaches are low GL, while pomegranates and rosemary are antioxidant champions!

1 Heat the butter in a skillet over low heat. Add the peaches and nectarines and heat through for 2 minutes. Add the fructose and leave to caramelize for 2 to 3 minutes.

2 Add the orange juice and rosemary and simmer until the liquid begins to thicken, 5 to 6 minutes. Remove the pan from the heat.

3 Meanwhile, cut the pomegranate into quarters and free the seeds from the bitter pith.

4 Divide the peaches and juice between 4 plates. Sprinkle the pomegranate seeds and pistachio nuts over the top.

PER SERVING GLYCEMIC LOAD 7; PROTEIN 5 G; CARBOHYDRATES 35 G; FAT 15 G (INCLUDES 5 G SATURATED FAT); FIBER 4 G

Passion Fruit Crème Brûlée

1 Preheat the oven to 300°F.

2 Halve the passion fruit and remove the contents with a spoon. Press the contents through a sieve, leaving the pits in the sieve.

2 Place the milk, cream, 3 tablespoons of the fructose, the cardamom, and passion fruit juice in a saucepan. Heat the mixture until the fructose has dissolved.

3 Whisk the eggs and egg yolks together in a bowl and pour in the hot milk mixture, stirring constantly. Pour the mixture back into the saucepan through a sieve to remove any threads of egg.

4 Pour the mixture into 4 ramekins placed in a roasting pan. Place the roasting pan in the oven and pour in about 4 cups hot water to make a water bath. Cook until the mixture begins to set, 30 to 40 minutes. Remove from the oven and let cool in the water bath. Place in the refrigerator for at least 1 hour.

5 Just before serving, sprinkle fructose over the surfaces and place under a hot broiler or use a blowtorch to caramelize the surface.

PER SERVING GLYCEMIC LOAD 4; PROTEIN 8 G; CARBOHYDRATES 19 G; FAT 19 G (INCLUDES 10 G SATURATED FAT); FIBER 1 G

◄ Blueberry Soup with Avocado Cream

It may sound like a strange combination, but you simply have to try this dessert—it's one of my favorites. Note that the cream contains uncooked egg.

SERVES 4

SOUP

4 cups blueberries

4 to 6 tablespoons fructose powder

2 tablespoons cornstarch

CREAM

1 ripe avocado

1 large egg

5 tablespoons unsweetened fromage blanc or quark

2 tablespoons fructose powder

1 tablespoon fresh lemon juice, or more, to taste

¼ teaspoon ground cinnamon

1 To make the soup, put the blueberries and fructose in a saucepan with 2 cups water and bring to a boil. Reduce the heat and simmer for 3 to 4 minutes. Dissolve the cornstarch in 3 tablespoons cold water and add to the soup, stirring constantly. Bring to a boil, then remove from the heat, and cool completely.

2 To make the cream, purée the avocado, egg, fromage blanc, fructose, lemon juice, and cinnamon in a blender until completely smooth.

3 Pour the blueberry soup into small bowls or soup plates and place a generous spoonful of avocado cream in each.

PER SERVING GLYCEMIC LOAD 9; PROTEIN 5 G; CARBOHYDRATES 48 G; FAT 9 G (INCLUDES 1.5 G SATURATED FAT); FIBER 7 G

Barley Pudding with Raspberry Sauce

This is made like a creamy rice pudding, but is better for your blood sugar level because barley has a lower GI than rice.

SERVES 4

PUDDING

¾ cup pearl barley

1 quart low-fat milk, or more, if needed

½ cinnamon stick

½ teaspoon salt

2 tablespoons fructose powder

¾ cup heavy cream

5 tablespoons unsweetened fromage blanc or quark

SAUCE

4 cups raspberries, fresh or frozen (thawed)

¼ cup fructose powder

1 Place the barley in a heavy saucepan with 1 cup water and bring to a boil over medium heat, stirring occasionally, until the water has been absorbed. Add the milk, cinnamon, and salt and lower the heat. Simmer, stirring occasionally and adjusting the heat so that the barley does not burn on the bottom of the pan. Cook until the barley is tender, about 25 minutes. If necessary, add more milk and cook for a bit longer. Transfer the pudding to a bowl, sprinkle with 2 teaspoons of the fructose, and leave to cool. Place in the refrigerator until completely cold.

2 Whisk the cream and the remaining 4 teaspoons fructose until thick and then stir in the fromage blanc and the barley pudding.

3 For the sauce, blend the raspberries with the fructose and then pass through a sieve.

4 Serve the barley pudding in bowls with the raspberry sauce poured on top or served separately.

PER SERVING GLYCEMIC LOAD 16; PROTEIN 15 G; CARBOHYDRATES 78 G; FAT 19 G (INCLUDES 12 G SATURATED FAT); FIBER 14 G

Cinnamon Parfaits with Marinated Berries

SERVES 6

PARFAITS

1¼ cups heavy cream

2 large eggs

2 large egg yolks

½ cup fructose powder

½ teaspoon ground cinnamon

8 ounces light cream cheese, softened

BERRIES

1 vanilla bean, split lengthwise

½ cinnamon stick

¼ cup fructose powder

4 cups fresh berries or 2 cups frozen

Serve with marinated or fresh berries or Raspberry Sauce (page 149). Note that the parfaits contain uncooked egg.

1 To make the parfaits, whisk the cream until stiff and place in the refrigerator. Whisk the eggs and egg yolks with the fructose until thick and pale yellow (this is best done in an electric mixer). Mix in the cinnamon. Stir the cream cheese to soften it and then mix it into the whipped cream. Carefully fold the cream mixture into the egg mixture.

2 Pour into 6 individual molds, bowls, or glasses. Cover with plastic wrap and freeze for at least 6 hours or overnight.

3 For the berries, place the vanilla, cinnamon, and fructose in a saucepan with 1 cup water and bring to a boil. Reduce the heat and simmer gently for 10 minutes. Pour the warm marinade over frozen berries or leave to cool to room temperature if using fresh berries. Leave the berries to marinate for at least 1 hour to allow the flavors to develop.

4 Remove the parfaits from the freezer 10 to 15 minutes before serving. Top with marinated berries.

PER SERVING GLYCEMIC LOAD 7; PROTEIN 8 G; CARBOHYDRATES 38 G; FAT 27 G (INCLUDES 16 G SATURATED FAT); FIBER 3.5 G

Raspberry Yogurt Sorbet

SERVES 4

2 cups frozen raspberries

½ cup fructose powder, or more, to taste

1 cup plain yogurt

1 tablespoon fresh lemon juice

This simple dessert takes just a few minutes to prepare. It can be made with any frozen berries; strawberries are also delicious.

1 Reserve a few berries for decoration. Combine the remaining berries, the fructose, yogurt, and lemon juice in a food processor and process to the desired consistency. The longer you process it, the thinner the sorbet will be.

2 Serve at once, in glass dishes. Decorate the top with frozen berries.

PER SERVING GLYCEMIC LOAD 7; PROTEIN 3 G; CARBOHYDRATES 35 G; FAT 2 G (INCLUDES 1 G SATURATED FAT); FIBER 4 G

Real Vanilla Ice Cream

SERVES 6

1¼ cups heavy cream
¾ cup whole milk
2 vanilla beans
5 large egg yolks
5½ tablespoons fructose powder
Pinch of salt

If you have an ice cream machine and an electric mixer, this luxurious ice cream is not difficult to make. For almond ice cream, use only one vanilla bean and add ½ cup lightly toasted chopped almonds to the chilled mixture before you freeze it.

1 Combine the cream and milk in a medium saucepan and bring to a boil.

2 Meanwhile, split the vanilla beans lengthwise and scrape out the seeds with a small knife. Add both the seeds and the pods to the cream mixture and place the pan over the lowest possible heat to infuse for about 20 minutes.

3 Whisk the egg yolks and fructose—ideally in a mixer—until light and airy. Remove the vanilla beans from the cream and whisk the cream gradually into the egg yolks. Pour the mixture back into the saucepan. Add the salt.

4 Return the pan to medium heat and heat the mixture, stirring constantly, until it has thickened enough to coat the back of a spoon; do not let it boil or it will curdle.

5 Strain the mixture into a bowl and let cool. When cold, place in the refrigerator until thoroughly chilled. Freeze in an ice cream maker. Transfer to an airtight container and store in the freezer.

PER SERVING GLYCEMIC LOAD 3; PROTEIN 4 G; CARBOHYDRATES 14 G; FAT 23 G (INCLUDES 13 G SATURATED FAT); FIBER 0 G

"Panna Cotta"

SERVES 4

1¼ cups low-fat milk
1 tablespoon honey
2 tablespoons fructose powder
¼ teaspoon ground cinnamon
1 packet (2½ teaspoons)
unflavored gelatin
⅔ cup fromage blanc
1 orange, peeled and diced
5 tablespoons chopped walnuts

This Italian dessert is traditionally made with cream, but to cut down on the fat I've substituted fromage blanc. Instead of the orange and walnuts, you could serve this with peaches, strawberries, or raspberries.

1 Place the milk, honey, fructose, and cinnamon in a saucepan. Bring slowly to a boil and simmer for about 5 minutes over low heat. Remove the pan from the heat.

2 Meanwhile, put the gelatin in a bowl, add a little water to moisten, and let sit for 5 minutes. Add to the milk and stir until the gelatin has completely dissolved. Let cool until just warm to the touch.

3 Add the fromage blanc and mix well, using a hand-held blender if desired. Pour the mixture into 4 glasses and leave to set in the refrigerator for at least 3 to 4 hours or overnight.

4 Mix the diced orange with the walnuts, sweeten to taste with a little fructose, and arrange on top of the panna cotta before serving.

PER SERVING GLYCEMIC LOAD 4; PROTEIN 9 G; CARBOHYDRATES 22 G; FAT 7 G (INCLUDES 1 G SATURATED FAT); FIBER 1.5 G

Pears Poached in Red Wine with Cardamom Sauce ▶

SERVES 4

SAUCE

⅔ cup fromage blanc or nonfat
Greek-style yogurt
¼ cup fructose powder
½ tablespoon ground cardamom
Juice of ½ lemon

PEARS

1 750 ml bottle red wine
3 tablespoons fructose powder
½ teaspoon ground cinnamon or 1
cinnamon stick
2 to 3 cardamom pods
4 pears, peeled
6 tablespoons chopped walnuts

1 To make the sauce, mix together the fromage blanc, fructose, cardamom, and lemon juice in a bowl. Cover and chill to allow the flavors to develop while you cook the pears.

2 In a deep saucepan, just large enough to hold the pears, bring the wine to a boil with the fructose, cinnamon, and cardamom. Reduce the heat and simmer for 5 minutes.

3 Add the pears and simmer until the pears are just tender when tested with a knife, 20 to 30 minutes, depending upon ripeness. Remove from the heat and let cool.

4 Lift the pears out of the wine with a slotted spoon and place on a serving dish. Strain the wine into a clean pan and boil until it thickens slightly, 5 to 10 minutes. Let cool and then pour over the pears.

5 To serve, sprinkle the pears with a few walnuts and pass the cardamom sauce separately at the table.

PER SERVING GLYCEMIC LOAD 8; PROTEIN 6 G; CARBOHYDRATES 51 G; FAT 7 G (INCLUDES 1 G SATURATED FAT); FIBER 6 G

Baked Apples with Vanilla Sauce

SERVES 4

SAUCE
½ vanilla bean
6 tablespoons fromage blanc,
quark, or Greek-style yogurt
¼ cup fructose powder
Juice of ½ lemon or lime

APPLES
4 apples
6 tablespoons chopped walnuts
¼ cup fructose powder
½ teaspoon ground cinnamon
1 tablespoon unsalted butter,
cut into pieces
½ cup sliced almonds, lightly
toasted

This recipe works just as well with pears. Instead of the vanilla, you could flavor the sauce with ground cinnamon or cardamom.

1 Preheat the oven to 350°F.

2 To make the vanilla sauce, split the vanilla bean and scrape out the contents with a small knife. Mix with the fromage blanc and stir in the fructose and lemon juice. Leave in the refrigerator for the flavors to develop.

3 Peel and core the apples and slice into 8 wedges each. Place in a baking dish. Sprinkle the walnuts, fructose, and cinnamon over the apples and mix well. Dot the surface with butter. Bake until the apples are tender when pierced with a knife, 20 minutes.

4 Sprinkle the almonds over the apples. Serve with the vanilla sauce on the side.

PER SERVING GLYCEMIC LOAD 10; PROTEIN 7 G; CARBOHYDRATES 48 G; FAT 16 G (INCLUDES 3 G SATURATED FAT); FIBER 5 G

Pear, Apple, and Apricot Compote

SERVES 6

2 cups dried apricots
2 pears
2 apples
Grated zest and juice of ½ lemon
¼ cup fructose powder
1 cinnamon stick
2 cloves
1 teaspoon cornstarch

Don't worry if you don't have all three fruits—just use extra of the fruits you do have. Serve cold, with yogurt or Vanilla Sauce (see above).

1 Soak the apricots in water overnight.

2 Peel and core the pears and apples. Cut each fruit into 8 wedges. Drain the apricots. Put all the fruit into a saucepan together with the lemon zest and juice, fructose, cinnamon, cloves, and 2 cups water. Bring to a boil, then reduce the heat, and simmer until the fruit is just tender, about 20 minutes.

3 Using a slotted spoon, transfer the fruit to a bowl and set aside to cool. Simmer the fruit juice for 10 minutes. Mix the cornstarch with 1 tablespoon water and stir into the juice. Bring to a boil, then strain the juice into a container and set aside to cool.

4 Pour the juice over the fruit.

PER SERVING GLYCEMIC LOAD 9; PROTEIN 1 G; CARBOHYDRATES 52 G; FAT 0 G (INCLUDES 0 G SATURATED FAT); FIBER 5 G

Wera's Fantastic Chocolate Cake

SERVES 12

CAKE

A little melted butter

4 cups ground almonds

1¾ ounces bittersweet chocolate

5 large eggs

½ cup fructose powder

2 tablespoons unsweetened cocoa powder

2 teaspoons baking powder

FILLING

7 tablespoons unsalted butter, at room temperature

½ cup fructose powder

1 teaspoon vanilla sugar

2 large egg yolks

TOPPING

1¾ ounces bittersweet chocolate

1 teaspoon vanilla sugar

1½ tablespoons unsalted butter

1 teaspoon instant coffee powder

Note that the filling contains uncooked egg yolks.

1 To make the cake, arrange a rack on the bottom shelf of the oven and preheat the oven to 325°F. Grease a 9-inch round, deep cake pan with melted butter.

2 Place the almonds and chocolate in a food processor and process until very fine.

3 Using an electric mixer, whisk the eggs and fructose until very thick and pale. Sift in the cocoa powder and baking powder and gently mix in the almonds and chocolate. Pour the mixture into the prepared pan and bake until a thin skewer inserted into the center of the cake comes out clean, about 30 minutes.

4 Use a knife to loosen the edges of the cake from the pan. Turn out onto a wire rack and let cool.

5 For the filling, beat the butter with the fructose and vanilla sugar until pale and fluffy. Beat in the the egg yolks.

6 For the topping, combine the chocolate, vanilla sugar, butter, and coffee powder with 1 tablespoon water in a small heatproof bowl and place over a saucepan of gently simmering water, stirring until the chocolate is melted and all the ingredients are well mixed. Set aside until lukewarm.

7 Slice the cake in half horizontally. Spread the filling on the bottom half. Cover with the other half of the cake and spread the chocolate glaze on top. Leave the cake in the refrigerator for 1 hour to set. Serve chilled, cut into slices.

PER SERVING GLYCEMIC LOAD 8; PROTEIN 11 G; CARBOHYDRATES 28 G; FAT 31 G (INCLUDES 9 G SATURATED FAT); FIBER 4 G

◄ Carrot Cake

SERVES 12

CAKE

3 large eggs
¾ cup fructose powder
½ cup canola oil
⅔ cup whole-wheat spelt flour
½ cup soy flour
⅓ cup ground almonds
2 teaspoons baking powder
½ teaspoon ground cinnamon
½ teaspoon ground ginger
¼ teaspoon salt
4 cups finely grated carrots
Scant ½ cup chopped walnuts

ICING

8 ounces light cream
cheese, softened
2 tablespoons fructose powder
1 tablespoon fresh lemon juice
½ teaspoon vanilla sugar

1 Preheat the oven to 350°F. Lightly oil a 9-inch cake pan.

2 Using an electric mixer, whisk the eggs and fructose until very thick and pale. Set the mixer to low speed and slowly pour in the oil. Add the spelt flour, soy flour, ground almonds, baking powder, cinnamon, ginger, and salt. Mix everything together well. Stir in the carrots and walnuts.

3 Put the mixture into the prepared pan. Bake until a thin skewer inserted into the center of the cake comes out clean, 40 to 50 minutes. Let the cake cool in the pan on a wire rack for 15 minutes. Turn the cake out of the pan and let cool completely.

4 To make the icing, stir together the cream cheese, fructose, lemon juice, and vanilla sugar. Coat the top and sides of the cake with the icing. Leave in the refrigerator for at least 1 hour before slicing and serving.

PER SERVING GLYCEMIC LOAD 9; PROTEIN 6 G; CARBOHYDRATES 26 G; FAT 18 G (INCLUDES 3 G SATURATED FAT); FIBER 3 G

Almond Tartlets with Cardamom Cream and Strawberries

SERVES 8

CRUST

3 tablespoons unsalted butter,
at room temperature,
plus extra for brushing
1½ cups whole almonds
2 tablespoons fructose powder
⅔ cup coarse rolled oats

FILLING AND TOPPING

5 tablespoons fromage blanc
1 tablespoon fructose powder
½ teaspoon vanilla sugar
¼ teaspoon ground cardamom
1 pint small fresh strawberries

1 Preheat the oven to 350°F. Grease 8 individual 4-inch tartlet pans by brushing them with melted butter.

2 To make the crust, grind the almonds—but not too finely—in a food processor with the fructose. Transfer to a bowl and stir in the butter and oats. Divide the pastry into 8 pieces and press into the tartlet pans. Bake until the pastry is firm and pale golden, 10 to 12 minutes. Let cool in the pans before unmolding. The crusts will be very brittle and must be handled carefully.

3 For the filling, mix the fromage blanc, fructose, vanilla sugar, and cardamom and spoon into the tartlet crusts. Halve the strawberries and arrange on the cardamom cream. Serve within 2 hours.

PER SERVING GLYCEMIC LOAD 5; PROTEIN 8 G; CARBOHYDRATES 19 G; FAT 19 G (INCLUDES 4 G SATURATED FAT); FIBER 4 G

GL list

These tables are compiled from information supplied by laboratories in various countries. There are many variables in testing methods, calculation data, and composition of food, and sometimes the result is the mean of several studies. Rice, for example, shows a large range of GL values; this variation is due to botanical differences in rice from country to country.

 The first column in the table gives the Glycemic Index. The second tells you the amount of food containing 50 grams (1¾ ounces) of carbohydrate: this is the amount of food used in laboratory tests to determine the GI. The third column is what I use to calculate the Glycemic Load (GL) of 100 grams (3½ ounces) of food, which you will find in the fourth column.

 When looking at the tables think of carbohydrates in terms of high, medium, or low GL—rather than being concerned with the specific numbers. I consider a GL of 20 or more as high, 11 to 19 as medium, and 10 and below as low.

Foods	GI	Amount of food in grams containing 50 g carbohydrate	Carbohydrate (grams) per 100 g of food	GL per 100 g (3½ ounces) of food
Apples	38	400	13	5
Apples, dried	29	88	57	16
Apple juice, unsweetened	40	431	12	5
Apricots	57	667	8	4
Apricots, dried	31	107	47	14
Apricots, canned, in light syrup	64	316	16	10
Bagel	72	100	50	36
Baguette	95	100	50	48
Banana	52	250	20	10
Barley, pearl	25	179	28	7
Barley porridge/wholemeal barley flour	68	179	28	19
Beans, baked	48	500	10	5
Beans, black, dried, boiled	20	300	17	3
Beans, borlotti (brown), dried, boiled	24	100	50	12
Beans, broad (fava), boiled	79	364	14	11
Beans, green, boiled	29	1667	8	2
Beans, kidney, dried, boiled	28	300	17	5
Beans, kidney, canned	52	441	11	6
Beans, lima, dried, boiled	32	250	20	6
Beans, lima, canned	36	335	15	5
Beans, mung, dried, boiled	31	441	11	4
Beans, mung, sprouts	25	441	11	3
Beans, navy, dried, boiled	38	242	21	8
Beans, pinto, dried, boiled	39	288	17	7
Beans, soy, dried, boiled	18	1250	4	1
Beans, soy, canned	14	1250	4	1
Beets	64	571	9	6
Bread, flat Middle Eastern	97	94	53	52
Bread, gluten free, white	76	100	50	38
Bread, hamburger bun	61	100	50	31
Bread, multi-grain	43	108	46	20
Bread, oat bran	47	83	60	28
Bread, pita	57	88	57	32
Bread, pumpernickel	50	125	40	20
Bread, rice	66	116	43	28
Bread, rye, dark (100% whole-wheat)	58	107	47	27
Bread, sourdough, white flour	54	107	47	25
Bread, soy and linseed	36	166	30	11
Bread, spelt, dark	63	79	63	40

Foods	GI	Amount of food in grams containing 50 g carbohydrate	Carbohydrate (grams) per 100 g of food	GL per 100 g (3½ ounces) of food
Bread, stone-ground whole-wheat	49	94	53	26
Bread, sunflower and barley	57	151	37	21
Bread, white	70	98	51	36
Bread, white flour, 80% whole-grain	52	75	67	35
Breadfruit	68	222	23	15
Buckwheat	54	250	20	11
Bulgur wheat	48	288	17	8
Carrot, boiled	58	667	8	4
Carrot, raw	16	500	10	2
Carrot juice	43	543	9	4
Cashew nuts	22	192	26	6
Cassava	46	185	27	12
Cereal, All-Bran (Kellogg's)	42	100	50	21
Cereal, bran flakes	74	83	60	44
Cereal, Cheerios	74	75	67	49
Cereal, Coco Pops (Kellogg's)	77	58	87	67
Cereal, cornflakes	81	58	87	70
Cereal, Frosted Flakes (Kellogg's)	55	58	87	48
Cereal, Grapenuts	71	71	70	50
Cereal, Just Right	60	64	78	47
Cereal, puffed wheat	74	71	70	52
Cereal, Shredded Wheat	75	76	66	49
Cereal, Special K (Kellogg's)	54	71	70	38
Cereal, Weetabix	70	79	63	44
Cherries	22	500	10	2
Chickpeas, dried, boiled	28	250	20	6
Chickpeas, canned	42	341	15	6
Chocolate, dark, 70% cacao	22	156	32	7
Chocolate, M & Ms, peanut	33	88	57	19
Chocolate, Mars	65	75	67	43
Chocolate, milk	43	89	56	24
Chocolate, Snickers	55	88	57	31
Chocolate, Twix	44	77	65	29
Corn, fresh	53	234	21	11
Corn, chips	63	96	52	33
Couscous, boiled	58	431	12	7
Cranberry juice	56	431	12	6
Crispbread	64	78	64	41
Croissant	67	110	46	31

Foods	GI	Amount of food in grams containing 50 g carbohydrate	Carbohydrate (grams) per 100 g of food	GL per 100 g (3½ ounces) of food
Dates, dried	103	75	67	69
Digestive biscuits	55	73	68	37
Doughnut	76	102	49	37
Fructose powder	19	50	100	19
Grapefruit	25	545	9	2
Grapefruit juice, unsweetened	48	625	8	4
Grapes	46	333	15	7
Glucose	100	50	100	100
Honey	55	69	72	40
Hummus	6	300	17	1
Ice cream, premium (15% fat)	37	278	18	7
Ice cream, low fat (1.2% – 7.1% fat)	43	227	22	9
Kiwi fruit	53	500	10	5
Lactose	46	50	100	46
Lentils, green, dried, boiled	30	441	11	3
Lentils, green, canned	52	454	11	6
Lentils, red, dried, boiled	26	417	12	3
Maltose	105	50	100	105
Mango	51	353	14	7
Marmalade, orange	48	75	67	32
Melon, orange-fleshed	65	1000	5	5
Milk, buttermilk	11	1136	4	0
Milk, full-fat	27	1042	5	1
Milk, low-fat	29	1000	5	1
Milk, skim	32	962	5	2
Milk, soy	42	714	7	3
Millet, boiled	71	208	24	17
Muffin	57	102	49	28
Muesli, sweetened	55	79	63	35
Muesli, unsweetened	49	76	66	32
Noodles, instant	47	225	22	10
Noodles, mung bean/transparent	33	200	25	8
Noodles, rice	61	231	22	13
Noodles, Chinese vermicelli	58	231	22	13
Oat cakes	57	79	63	36
Oranges	42	545	9	4
Orange juice, unsweetened	46	481	10	5
Papaya	59	353	14	8
Parsnip, boiled	97	333	15	15

Foods	GI	Amount of food in grams containing 50 g carbohydrate	Carbohydrate (grams) per 100 g of food	GL per 100 g (3½ ounces) of food
Pasta, brown rice, boiled	92	237	21	19
Pasta, corn, boiled	54	214	23	13
Pasta, fettucine (durum wheat), boiled	40	196	26	10
Pasta, gnocchi (potato-based)	68	188	27	18
Pasta, macaroni, boiled	47	188	27	13
Pasta, spaghetti, al dente	39	191	26	10
Pasta, spaghetti, boiled 10–15 mins	43	188	27	11
Pasta, spaghetti, protein-rich/low-carb, boiled	27	173	29	8
Pasta, spaghetti, whole-wheat, boiled	37	214	23	9
Peaches	42	545	9	4
Peaches, canned, in juice	38	545	9	3
Peanuts	14	417	12	2
Pears	38	545	9	3
Pears, canned, in juice	43	545	9	4
Peas, black-eyed, dried, boiled	42	250	20	8
Peas, green, fresh	48	571	9	4
Peas, yellow split (chana dal)	11	208	24	3
Pineapple	59	462	11	6
Pineapple juice, unsweetened	46	357	14	6
Pizza (average of 5 toppings, GI varies from 30 to 80)	60	185	27	16
Plums	39	500	10	4
Polenta, boiled	68	577	9	6
Popcorn	72	91	55	40
Porridge, made from oat bran	55	500	10	5
Porridge, made from rolled oats	58	568	9	5
Porridge, instant	66	481	10	7
Potato, baked in skin	85	250	20	17
Potato, boiled, peeled	88	417	12	11
Potato, boiled, unpeeled	80	441	11	10
Potato, chips	54	102	42	23
Potato, french fries	75	259	19	15
Potato, instant, mashed	85	375	13	11
Potato, mashed	74	375	13	10
Potato, new, boiled in skin	57	357	14	8
Potato, new, canned	63	417	12	8
Potatoes, steamed	65	278	18	18
Prunes, pitted, ready-to-eat	29	91	55	16
Pumpkin, boiled	75	1000	5	4

Foods	GI	Amount of food in grams containing 50 g carbohydrate	Carbohydrate (grams) per 100 g of food	GL per 100 g (3½ ounces) of food
Quinoa	35	294	17	6
Raisins	64	68	73	47
Ravioli, with meat	39	237	21	8
Rice, basmati, white	58	197	25	15
Rice, basmati, precooked in pouch	57	185	27	15
Rice, brown	55	227	22	12
Rice, jasmine	109	179	28	31
Rice, parboiled/converted (Uncle Ben's)	47	208	24	11
Rice, risotto/arborio	69	143	35	24
Rice, white, long-grain	56	183	27	15
Rice, white, long-grain, Bangladeshi	38	192	26	10
Rice, wild	57	238	21	12
Rice cakes	91	60	83	76
Rutabaga	72	750	7	5
Rye, whole-grain, boiled	34	66	76	26
Scones	92	139	36	33
Soda, Coca Cola	58	481	10	6
Soda, orange (Fanta)	68	368	14	9
Sponge cake	54	95	53	29
Sports drink (Gatorade)	78	833	6	5
Strawberries	40	2000	3	1
Sugar (sucrose)	68	50	100	68
Sweet potatoes, cooked	61	268	19	11
Taco shells, corn	68	83	60	41
Tomato juice	38	1389	4	1
Tortilla, corn, fresh	52	104	48	25
Watermelon	72	1000	5	4
Wheat, whole-grain, boiled	41	74	68	28
Yam	66	208	24	16
Yogurt, fat-free, natural, unsweetened	33	625	8	3
Yogurt, fat-free, soy, with fruit and sugar	50	385	13	7
Yogurt, fat-free, with aspartame	14	769	7	1
Yogurt, fat-free, with fruit and sugar	33	323	16	5
Yogurt, low-fat, with fruit and sugar	33	303	16	5
Yogurt, low-fat, with fruit and aspartame	14	862	6	1

Frequently
asked questions

Q **How does Eating the Greek Way differ from low-carb diets?**

A Most low-carb diets severely restrict the intake of carbohydrates in order to encourage the body to burn fat. Although Eating the Greek Way means you will consume fewer carbohydrates than many people are used to, it is not low carb but "slow" carb.

The theory behind diets that severely limit or omit carbohydrates altogether is that when the body does not have a sufficient supply of glucose (which is provided by carbohydrates), it has to burn fat as an energy source. This process, known as ketosis, begins about 24 hours after no carbohydrates have been eaten. Breaking down body fat leads to the formation of substances called ketones, which the body can use as energy instead of blood sugar to a certain extent. Although this sort of approach will result in short-term weight loss, it is not a balanced or healthy long-term diet. Not only does it give you bad breath, but more importantly it causes you to lose fluids and important minerals—which you would then need to replace with supplements—through increased urination.

My aim is to provide a balanced, sensible diet, based on both traditional wisdom and cutting-edge scientific knowledge, that you can—and more importantly that you will want to—follow for the rest of your life. It is designed to restore a more natural balance of the types of carbohydrates, proteins, and fats you eat. Therefore I do not advocate going through different steps or phases with severe restriction of any food. I want you to improve your health and weight permanently. This means eating more natural foods and fewer refined and processed foods. This is particularly relevant with regard to carbohydrates, because the type of carbohydrate we eat affects our blood sugar levels and these are closely connected with hunger, cravings and the extent to which we store or burn fat. Slow carbs cause a gradual rise in blood sugar levels while processed carbs cause it to spike, which can lead to a myriad of health problems.

So, although carbs in general have acquired a tarnished image recently, there is no need to deny yourself them altogether—simply choose wisely. The GL list on pages 159–63 is designed to help you do just that. And don't forget that your choice of healthy, minimally processed fats is extremely important, too.

Q **You mention inflammation frequently—isn't this a minor problem, unconnected to diet?**

A You may be surprised to learn that inflammation is in fact involved in every type of chronic disease. Inflammation is a natural and necessary reaction: when you get a sprain or burn the affected area becomes red and swollen. This is caused by hormone-like substances called eicosanoids, whose job it is to fight the assault. However, under certain conditions, inflammation can become chronic and exacerbate an existing condition or cause chronic disease.

Chronic inflammation means that something has gone very wrong with your health. Instead of repairing your body—which is the purpose of localized, temporary inflammation—chronic inflammation breaks it down, speeds up the aging process and causes disease. Inflammatory diseases have increased dramatically in recent decades, in tandem with the increased consumption of omega-6-rich vegetable oils, trans fatty acids, and the processed foods containing them. These so-called pro-inflammatory foods are known to encourage inflammation and should be avoided. Increasing your intake of anti-inflammatory foods decreases inflammation and promotes good health. Omega-3 fatty acids (found in oily fish, flaxseed oil, and to a lesser degree in nuts) and antioxidant-rich foods such as vegetables and fruit, berries and herbs, nuts and seeds are anti-inflammatory.

Q **Do you advocate the use of supplements?**

A First let me point out that having a well-balanced and varied diet is the best thing you can do to achieve good health; supplements are not magic bullets that can make you well if your lifestyle is unhealthy. Too many people put their faith in vitamin and mineral supplements when they need to put more effort into eating properly.

That said, many of us are likely to need special supplements at certain times, for example because of illness or when pregnant or breastfeeding. Vegans need to take vitamin B12, as this vitamin is only found in animal food sources; vegetarians can obtain vitamin B12 from eggs, cheese, and milk.

However, it could also be argued that a multivitamin and mineral supplement is an inexpensive health insurance premium for most people. The reasoning behind this is that in the modern world we are all subject to environmental pollutants and stress, which can increase our bodies' needs for additional vitamins and minerals; also, much of the food we eat today no longer has the same nutritional value it once did (due to modern farming methods, soil depletion, long-distance shipping of produce, and so on).

If you feel dietary supplements are appropriate for you, I suggest you discuss it with your doctor, as some are contra-indicated if you are taking other medications.

Q How do I overcome my cravings for sweet and starchy foods?

A Ensure you eat regularly and in particular don't miss breakfast or your mid-morning and late-afternoon snacks, as these are important in keeping the blood sugar balanced (they are also the meals that people most often skip). If you miss breakfast it is virtually guaranteed that by mid-morning your body will be craving whatever will raise your blood sugar fastest—and that's sweet, highly refined carbs! The same goes for your snacks. It is also important to include protein in every meal and snack, as protein is more satiating than carbohydrate alone. If you opt for fruit in order to satisfy your need for something sweet, this should also be accompanied by protein—for example some nuts.

Eating the Greek Way should reduce your appetite for sweet or starchy foods, as you will not be subject to the same swings in blood sugar that often cause cravings. However, if you continue to suffer from cravings you may want to try the supplement 5-HTP (5-hydroxytryptophan). It has been proven to suppress appetite, especially the craving for sweets and starches. The effect is probably due to the fact that 5-HTP increases the level of serotonin, the brain chemical that has a soothing, calming effect. Several foods, including sugar and chocolate, are known to increase the level of serotonin in the brain. 5-HTP is produced in the body from tryptophan, an amino acid found in most protein foods. A well-balanced diet that includes sufficient protein in all meals will ensure an adequate intake of 5-HTP under normal circumstances.

There have been no reports of serious side effects, though drowsiness may occur if taken during the day, and it is not suitable for pregnant or lactating women. Start by taking 25 to 50 milligrams approximately one hour before bedtime a couple of times a week. Then gradually increase the number of nights you take it, until you take it every night. It is important not to buy a food supplement that contains other ingredients in addition to 5-HTP. Some of these supplements may contain Ephedra (or the Chinese herb Ma Huang, containing Ephedra), which has been linked to serious side effects and should be avoided.

Q The GL of some foods is higher than I expected. Oat cakes are a good example—they appear to have a high GL of 36 when I thought they were medium or low GL. Can you explain?

A I present the GL of foods per 100 grams, not per serving size. This allows for easy comparison between foods and is similar to the way nutritional labels are presented. It is therefore important that you consider the size of the portion you eat. The GL of 100 g (3$\frac{1}{2}$ ounces) of oat cakes may be high, but that is equal to about 10 oat cakes—a lot more than most people would eat in a normal serving. If you were to eat 2 oat cakes, the GL would be 7, which is much more acceptable.

Remember, however, that this principle works in reverse, too. A 100 g (3½-ounce) serving of cooked pasta may have a medium GL of around 13 but many people eat far larger portions; if you eat 200 g (7 ounces) the GL will be 26. This is why portion control is such an important part of weight loss. The best way to achieve portion control without having to count grams or calories is to focus on food choices and the composition of your plate, and by eating frequent low-glycemic meals and snacks. The satiety this provides regulates appetite and leads to automatic control of total food intake.

Q What is fructose and why do you recommend its use?

A Fructose is the form of sugar found in all fruit. It is 30 to 50 percent sweeter than ordinary sugar (it tastes sweeter in powder form than in liquid form), so you use 30 to 50 percent less to obtain the same level of sweetness and hence take in fewer calories. Fructose also causes considerably less tooth decay. Most importantly, fructose is absorbed more slowly and cannot be converted into energy immediately; hence it has a low GI of 19.

That does not mean you should use it in unlimited quantities. You should reduce your intake of all types of sugar, but use small amounts of fructose where necessary instead of ordinary sugar. I use it where a little sweetness is required in a savory recipe or when I'm baking the occasional sweet treat. When adapting your own recipes, you will need about one-third less fructose than sugar. For baking, reduce the oven temperature by around 125°F and bake for slightly longer than you would for recipes containing sugar.

You'll find fructose in powder form in the baking aisle of the supermarket, or in health food shops. It is more expensive than sucrose—which is partly why the food industry has shunned it in favor of sucrose—but it is worth the extra expense. Pure

fructose powder is not the same as high-fructose corn syrup or HFCS, which is used in many processed foods and sweetened drinks. HFCS is almost identical to regular sugar (sucrose), but comes in liquid form and is derived from maize. HFCS is high-glycemic and should be avoided.

Q Why does honey have a high GI if it contains fructose?

A Honey is a water solution of glucose and fructose in varying proportions: It does not have a standard GI because it is not a standard product. The GI of honey varies according to the ratio of glucose to fructose; the more fructose, the lower the GI. I have heard, but cannot verify, that the thinner the honey, the more fructose it contains. If so, this suggests that thin honey might be better than thicker honey.

Q Peanuts have a low GI. Would that be fresh peanuts or salted?

A All peanuts have the same GI, but raw peanuts are a much healthier option than salted or dry roasted, both because of the salt and other additives, and because the peanut fat is heated during roasting/processing.

Q When they are in season, I eat strawberries almost every day. Will this affect my blood sugar levels?

A All berries have a low GI. Strawberries have such a low carbohydrate content that their GI is almost insignificant, so you can eat as many strawberries as you like with a clear conscience. Try raspberries, too—they are particularly rich in fiber and vitamin C. You could add some natural yogurt or cottage cheese to your berries for a better protein balance.

Q How is GI affected by heating? I know that foods such as potatoes have a higher GI when they are cooked but what about other foods, such as rice?

A No general rule applies here. However, foods rich

in starch, such as potatoes, carrots, turnips. and other root vegetables often get a higher GI when they are cooked because the starch they contain is converted from amylose to amylopectin (of the two types of starch, amylopectin has the higher GI). Vegetables which are not high in starch do not have an increased GI when cooked. The GI of rice increases with cooking time: Generally the stickier the rice, the higher the GI. This is why jasmine rice has a higher GI than long-grain basmati.

Q I like to bake—what are the alternatives to white flour?

A Instead of white flour, choose stone-ground whole-wheat flour. Soy flour, which is very high in protein and has a low GI, can be used to replace about one third to a half of the white flour in most recipes. You can also use oat flour or flour from ancient wheat types such as spelt and kamut; the latter contain more vitamins, minerals, and protein than regular wheat flour. Try using them instead of a proportion of white flour. Also remember that the more nuts and seeds you use in a bread, the lower its glycemic effect and the healthier it becomes.

When baking cakes, you can if you wish replace all the white flour with one-third soy flour, one-third barley flour, and one-third finely ground almonds. You may have to adjust the amount of liquid in the recipe to achieve the same result that you do with regular flour. It takes some experimenting, but it's worth the effort.

Q I drink a lot of coffee. Should I avoid caffeine altogether or will cutting back be sufficient? Is tea any better?

A The issue of whether or not coffee is healthy is a contentious one. There has actually been quite a bit of research that has shown favorable results. Coffee drinkers, for example, appear to suffer less from asthma, and caffeine is associated with a lower risk of developing Parkinson's disease. Even more importantly, a number of large studies have shown that those with a moderate intake of coffee have about a 40 percent lower risk of developing type 2 diabetes. Coffee is, in fact, one of the most significant sources of antioxidants in Western diets, mainly because coffee consumption is so high.

On the negative side, coffee has been found to increase homocysteine levels in the blood, which is associated with a greater risk of Alzheimer's and cardiovascular disorders. However, there is no direct evidence of a connection between coffee drinking and these disorders. Coffee has also been shown to impair fertility among non-smoking women. In addition, it contains acrylamide and cadmium, potentially carcinogenic substances.

There is no doubt that coffee also provides pleasure, so taking the above into account I recommend moderation rather than abstinence or excess. Limit yourself to one or two cups of regular coffee a day or choose Swiss water-processed (naturally) decaffeinated coffee instead.

Black tea also contains caffeine. A far better choice is green tea, which is packed with even more antioxidants than black tea or coffee. Some of the antioxidants have been found to be more powerful than vitamins C and E. Green tea drinkers seem to have a lower risk of a wide range of diseases, from simple infections to chronic degenerative conditions, including cardiovascular disease, cancer, and osteoporosis.

Whatever your beverage of choice, bear in mind that the most important source of fluid for the body is water. Aim to drink at least 8 cups of water a day.

Q I often eat out at restaurants. Will the Eating the Greek way fit in with my lifestyle?

A It is becoming much easier to eat healthy food in all sorts of restaurants. The key is to bear in mind the general guidelines of this approach to eating. Probably the most practical approach is to make your restaurant meal your reward meal of that day. This will allow you to enjoy some carbohydrate such as potatoes, pasta or rice, or a dessert. The following general guidelines will also help:

- Have a small snack before you arrive at the restaurant so that you're not so ravenously hungry that you will eat anything. The snack should be high protein and high fiber (nuts and fruit for example).
- Avoid the bread basket. All bread is medium or high GI and will increase your blood sugar and insulin and even your appetite.
- If possible, opt for a salad dressed with vinaigrette as your starter, as this will lower the GL of the rest of the meal (this is because acidic foods such as vinegar and lemon juice have the effect of slowing down carbohydrate absorption). If you choose a soup, avoid thick creamy ones and opt for those based on clear broth.
- Avoid anything that is battered or deep-fried. If it isn't obvious how a dish is cooked, then ask.
- Restaurants offer a great opportunity to increase

your intake of fish, which most people don't eat enough of. Steamed, grilled, baked, or lightly stir-fried fish and seafood is great, but avoid fish cakes and breaded, battered, or crumbed dishes.
- If you opt for meat as your source of protein, choose poultry or lean cuts of meat and avoid processed meats such as sausages, pâté, and pies.
- Eat plenty of vegetables and don't forget legumes, which are a wonderfully healthy way of filling up.
- Be aware of portion sizes, particularly when having the carbohydrate part of your reward meal. Remember it should be half the size of your palm.
- If you are having dessert, choose one based on dairy products, eggs, and/or nuts rather than one made with flour.

Index

Recipe index